View of Sumner about 1891
Presbyterian church in center of photograph, Ryan Hall is left of church,
and Whitworth Collage is far center right, partially obscured.

THE SUMNER STORY
by one of her daughters

Amy M. Ryan

Sumner, Washington
1853 - 1900

2nd edition

Copyright © 1988, 2024 Sumner Historical Society (Sumner, WA)

Portions of this book originally appeared in *The Seattle Times, Tacoma News Tribune,* and *The Sumner News Index.*

This book was printed in the United States of America.

It has been produced in association with Firebird Creative LLC. (Clackamas, OR).

THE SUMNER STORY

TABLE OF CONTENTS

Foreword 1

Acknowledgments 3

Introduction 5

First Settlers 7

Life in 1870s 21

Hop Boom 29

Whitworth College Begins 34

Temperance Issues 38

Hardship for Pioneer Women 44

Quotes from Early Letters 51

Early Industries 56

Ryan's Hall or The Old Opera House 67

People of the Town 71

Early Schools 74

Early Churches 80

Entertainment 83

Decoration Day 91

Pioneer Cemetary 94

Main Street 97

Home Life in the 1890s 108

Whitworth Gave More Than His Name to College 114

U. W.'s First Graduate Has Exemplary Life 118

Redondo—It Will Always Be Called "Stone's Landing" by Many Old Timers 121

Photos 124

Index 143

FOREWORD

This history of Sumner, Washington, was written by Amy M. Ryan as a weekly *Sumner News Index* column during 1963-65. The Sumner Historical Society proudly published this history as a 1988-89 Centennial project. Several of Mrs. Ryan's historical articles which appeared between 1961 and 1963 in *The Seattle Times* and the *Tacoma News Tribune*, are also included, reprinted with permission.

Mrs. Ryan always had an interest in the history of the Puyallup Valley area. She felt accounts of the early days should be preserved and she spent her last years writing that story.

Amy M. Johns was born in Farmington, Iowa, in 1878, and when she was thirteen moved west to the Puyallup Valley with her family. She attended grade school in Auburn, Washington, then known as Slaughter. After her family moved to Sumner in 1891, she began attending Whitworth College because the public school had only three years of high school. At eighteen she passed the teachers' examination and received a certificate to teach third grade. She taught in Sumner and Fern Hill until she married Harry Roger Ryan in 1902. They lived in Spokane twenty years, then returned to Sumner where she lived until her death in 1967. She began writing at seventy years of age and continued until a few weeks before her death at age 88. Her vivid memory of the past, her extensive research, and the personal interviews with other old-time friends and relatives, made this history possible.

ACKNOWLEDGEMENTS

I thank the editor of the *Sumner News Index* for his courtesy and all my friends for their kindness in appreciation of my column. I would pay tribute to my sister-in-law, Edith Ryan Van Vechten, who passed away in September of this year (1965). Her contributions were invaluable and she enjoyed assisting in gathering notes for the history. Without her help I never could have done what we accomplished in getting accurate data for the articles.

I also wish to thank others who told me pioneer stories and loaned me abstracts and diaries for research. Thank you everyone.

Amy M. Ryan, 1965

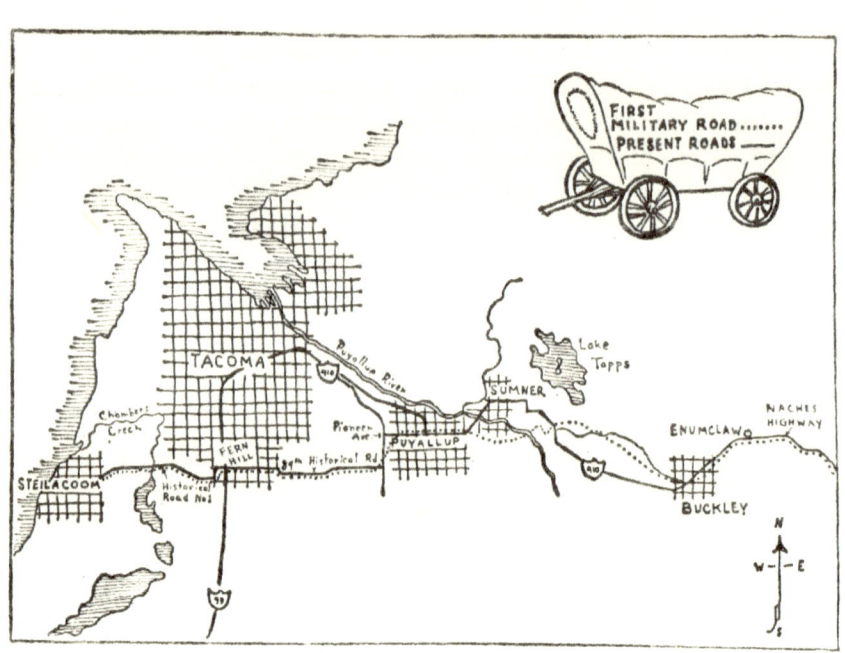

INTRODUCTION

"WHY DOESN'T someone write a history of Sumner!" has been the cry for many years. With much trepidation I am going to attempt to do that very thing, with a short article each week in the *Sumner News-Index*, thanks to the kind indulgence of the editor.

An old adage reads, "Fools rush in where angels fear to tread." I recall my good friend E. D. Swezey, a professor of languages in Whitworth College, warning me never to write history. He said if I did that inaccuracies would be pointed out and I would be embarrassed.

We came to Sumner in the fall of 1891. I believe my memories along with gleanings from old letters, diaries, *Sumner Herald*s, and interviews with descendants of pioneers will prove interesting.

I shall write in the first person in a conversational manner and endeavor to be true to facts, giving credit to the source of my information, hoping it will benefit Sumner.

In this day of the whirring of planes overhead, the roar of logging trucks, the purring of automobiles gliding over paved streets, it is hard to visualize this valley as it must have been before civilization came.

Historians relate the cataclysmic changes that came to the Northwest, perhaps millions of years ago. Mountains emerged from the water-covered terrain, not only once but again and again. Seeds sprouted, forests grew, then were inundated by glaciers and floods. In our library there are books which describe the many interesting glaciation of the Puget Sound country.

This has been proven true by the white glacier water that still flows through our rivers, which in the interglacial epoch frequently changed courses, sometimes flowing north and sometimes flowing south. This carved the deep troughs which we call valleys. Forest beds were buried far beneath silt brought by glaciers, sea shells were left on mountains high above sea level; all proving that at one time the whole Northwest was covered by water.

When the first settlers came and dug their wells and set fence posts, they found huge trees buried 12 feet down. In 1891 the *Sumner Herald* tells of C. A. Ryan Sr. discovering this when he fenced the property he had bought in Slaughter. Sam Burr and George H. Ryan encountered the same difficulty in the 1870s.

But most remarkable is that our city workers digging for the new sewer system in 1963 found an immense stump over 12 feet below the surface in the lower south Sumner district. They also dug into a layer of peat far below the gravel. When Dewey Coffman took some home and spread it over his garden, seeds sprouted which had been buried for no one knows how many years. He said you could almost trace the shape of the leaves which had rotted to make the peat.

After eons of change the valleys were left undisturbed, the tides kept their bounds and the rivers followed their courses. (One exception was when White River was diverted into the Stuck causing a rift between the two towns. White River ran right through the heart of Slaughter, now Auburn.)

When settlers came to our valley, it was a dense forest. Lacy mosses decorated the trees making it a veritable fairyland of beauty. There were no roads, no bridges, no Naches Pass over the mountains and only a few Indian trails as the Puget Sound Indians lived on sea food almost altogether and did very little hunting in the forest.

By erosion a few gravel pits had been exposed which gave clues to the geologists who tell us the story of what had taken place when the Cascade Mountains were lifted and hoary Mt. Rainier raised its head above the clouds. The Northwest was God's country then, man had not spoiled its primeval beauty.

CHAPTER 1
FIRST SETTLERS

Explorers came seeking the Northwest Passage. The Indians called them "white birds" which looked and sailed away. Among them were Sir Francis Drake, Capt. George Vancouver, Capt. Robert Gray and Capt. James Cook.

They were followed by the Hudson's Bay men, who often married Indian women, later leaving them and their children. This kindled a fire of resentment in the hearts of the redmen. Great Britain and the United States government had much controversy over which should have the rich Northwest country.

Land was offered by the U. S. government free to any white man, 21, and a citizen, if he would live on it and improve it. Thinking about this I wondered how Uncle Sam secured land to give away, thus holding it for him.

This took me to the encyclopedia where I found that when the *Declaration of Independence* was signed in 1776 the government owned no land. In 1780 states were asked to surrender areas of land claimed by them. In 1802 all western lands not privately owned were turned over to the federal government. The expansion of the new nation across the continent began.

The Louisiana purchase was concluded for $15,000,000 in 1803; Florida ceded by Spain for payment of $6,000,000; to Mexico $15,000,000 went for Texas in 1845 and $7,000,000 to Russia for Alaska in 1867. Texas, when she joined the union in 1845, withheld the right to dispose of her free land.

When a treaty was signed with Great Britain in 1846 setting the boundary between Canada and the Northwest, the influx of settlers began. The former is background for our history in Puyallup Valley.

The first settlers coming to the Northwest followed the Columbia River to Portland and then worked their way north to Thurston County and on to the prairie at Steilacoom.

When they saw Indians riding over the mountains on horseback they felt that a passage through the mountains was a possibility. Robert S. More wrote an interesting account of the cutting of the Naches Pass. He was one of the men who accomplished this difficult task. He says:

> The men who cut a road across the mountains through the Naches Pass were A. J. Allen, foreman, Robert Patterson, Smith, Miller, Lewis brothers, John Mills, James Barron, A. J. Burge, packer, Ephraim Allen, Henry

Allen, W. D. Van Buren, Thomas Rickson, Edward Gross Frasure, John Walker, James Boice, R. S. More, James Meeks. All were from Olympia and Steilacoom and a braver and more hard-working crew of men never existed.

We cut the road to the summit of the Naches, commencing at Boise Creek and thence to the summit. From thence to where the military road crosses at Van Ogles. Thence by the present road to the Kelly place and to South Prairie. We commenced cutting the road from Boise Creek to Montgomery's the fifteenth of June, 1853.

We were three and one-half months opening the road to the summit. Three and one half months of as hard work as men ever did. It took nerve and courage as we knew nothing of the country through which we were to go.

About the fourth or fifth of October while we were camped at the Puyallup River opposite the present Van Ogle place, at midnight there came across the river a loud "Hello!" We were startled for we did not know of any whites in our rear. When we answered we were told there were 70 immigrants behind and that they were short of provisions.

Jonathan W. McCarty wrote for the *Tacoma Ledger* of the harrowing experiences the members of the wagon train had experienced. He tells of oxen becoming frightened, running away, wrecking the wagons, Indians stealing their cattle, storms causing stampedes of animals, ferrying rivers and shortage of food.

James Longmire in *Told by the Pioneers* goes into more detail of the hardships encountered.

At Orando Ronde a happy surprise awaited us. Nelson Sargent whose father was in our party, had met John Lane, who had arrived in advance of us, with the welcome news that a party of workmen had started out from Olympia and Steilacoom to make a road for us through the Naches Pass over the Cascades, our being the first party of immigrants to attempt a crossing of the Columbia River north of The Dallas. Lane waited for us and with E. A. Light and others continued with our party.

From Steilacoom Edward Allen wrote:

Sixty-eight times the wagon train crossed the Naches river. It was slow traveling, some days but three miles were made and at one place they were forced to travel 50 miles without food for the animals other than browsing from bushes at the roadside. Everybody, men, women and children of 10 years and more worked on the road. Trees were cut, rocks and stones removed, tunnels were driven beneath great logs to let the wagons through, or with small logs, with earth and stones the weary workers built runways to carry their wagons over fir and cedar logs.

Traveling up the canyon of Naches had been hard; but the descent of the western slope was worse. At the summit, barefooted children in tattered clothing shivered in the frost-laden air of October mornings. Food supplies were almost exhausted, but now that they had reached the summit, the immigrants took new hope. Lean cattle and bony horses were hitched to the wagons containing the little property saved from the long trip; much had been thrown away to lighten the loads. Leaving the summit glades the train set out down the new road. The first day's travel brought it to what one of the women called "the jumping off place"—the edge of a great bluff too steep for descent by ordinary methods.

A consultation was held and it was decided to lower the wagons with ropes. The available ropes were too short. Women wept and men cursed and then James Biles said, "Kill one of the poorest of my steers, make a rope of his hide and see if that will be long enough. If not, kill another."

Three lean, starved steers were required before the right length of rope was made. This was passed around trees and the wagons were lowered down the steepest part of the hill to a place where the cattle could be hitched to them.

Rough locked and with pieces of knotty logs attached as drags, they were taken down to camp at the first crossing at Greenwater. For two days men and women and animals labored on the hill by a circuitous route through the woods.

One of the parties, composed of Mrs. James Longmire and Mrs. E. A. Light with their children, were suddenly confronted by a man who exclaimed, "My God, women, where did you come from? Are there any more of you?" The man was Andrew Burge, in charge of the transportation of supplies to the men in the road camp.

Burge told the immigrants it would be almost impossible for them to make their way over the road to the settlements and advised them to return to the eastern side of the mountains. But having come thus far the travelers were not disposed to take this advice and continued on down the hill, across the Greenwater and at last arrived at Steilacoom.

Not a day passed but some animal fell by the wayside and died of starvation. Among the exhausted animals was a fine thoroughbred Kentucky mare belonging to G. H. Baker. It was decided the most humane thing to do under the circumstances was to kill her, to relieve her of further suffering. Mrs. Baker, hearing of the plan refused to permit the execution, remained with her and after great search and exertion succeeded in getting food from the surrounding woods, and water from the stream.

All day the devoted woman remained with the beautiful mare and later brought her into camp.

A few days later the incident was repeated and again Mrs. Baker refused to allow the fatal shot to be fired, again saved the mare's life and finally brought her to the American settlement. Many local famous race horses of Oregon and Washington trace their ancestry to this Kentucky mare.

Among the immigrants was Tyrus Himes, wife and four children, the oldest of whom was George H. Himes, secretary of the Oregon Historical Society, then a boy of 10. Crossing the White River on a foot log, the men were busy getting the animals across and left the women and children to shift for themselves. One end of the log swayed up and down in the current and, as the 10-year-old boy helped his younger brother and two sisters and his mother across, Mrs. Himes lost control of her nerves and fell into the raging river, still holding on to her son. He grabbed hold of an overhanging branch and finally got her safely over.

This long weary trek down the mountain took several days during which the animals lived on late fall leaves and vine maple.

James Longmire writes:

We bridged huge logs by cutting others and laying them alongside so we could get the wagons over. Finally all except John Lane, E. A. Light and myself left their wagons, because of their failing oxen, which they drove before them to the prairie where there was good grass. We at last reached what later became Van Ogle's farm and found the river filled with humpbacked salmon and as the river was low we went after them with clubs and axes. What a feast we had after living on potatoes without even salt! My wife being indisposed could not eat the fish and bought a pheasant from an Indian, the first purchase on Puget Sound.

From *Told By the Pioneers* we get the list of those in the party who came over Naches in 1853. The foregoing shows us of what stuff these pioneers were made and the heritage which is ours because of this wonderful valley settled by some of them, who took donation claims where Sumner now is located.

James Longmire gives this list in his narrative of the trip: William M. Kincaid, his children, Ruth Kincaid, Susannah Kincaid, John Kincaid, Chris Kincaid, James Kincaid, Laura Kincaid and Joseph Kincaid, all from Kentucky; Isaac Woolery, Mrs. Isaac Woolery, Robert L. Woolery, James M. Woolery, Sarah Jane (she was born on the way west), Abraham Woolery, Mrs. A. Woolery (Aunt Pop), Jacob Francis Woolery, Daniel Woolery, Agnes Woolery, from Missouri. These are the members of the first 1853 Naches trek who located where Sumner began.

William M. Kincaid's wife was Nancy Woolery, (deceased) sister of A. and I. Woolery, so it was two related families who first settled Sumner.

Our readers may be interested in more incidents which took place on the journey over the plains. How hard it was for the women to decide what to bring when they did not know what the future held for them in the new country where they hoped to find a home.

How they studied what to pack in the wagons which were to be their homes for seven long months! Some managed to crowd in a few treasured pieces of walnut furniture. But when the tired oxen refused to pull such a load when food became scarce, discarded tables, whatnots, shelves, cupboards left along the trail, spoke eloquently of the sacrifices made by the women to lighten the loads.

The women and children ran ahead and gathered spears of grass to feed the oxen, buffalo chips for fuel when a halt was made for the night and fires had to be made to cook meals. How did they manage to keep clean when there was no water except when they came to a river! Then washings had to be done in water heated over an open fire.

Fording these rivers often brought tragedies. We can never know of the hardships endured by these early settlers, and the ever-constant fear of marauding Indians. When camped at night the women wrapped their featherbeds around their children for protection.

"Aunt Pop," as she was affectionately called because she kept up the morale of the company by her cheerfulness, held a man at bay with an ox-goad when he tried to take a piece of meat from provisions which had been brought by scouts and was left in her care until it could be evenly divided by the two oldest men of the party. He said, "I'm hungry," and she replied, "I'm hungry too, but we are going to wait until the proper ones come to divide it evenly." I remember her as a little old lady and she did not seem like a brave person in the 1890s. However, this story is true.

After pouring over ancient abstracts, deciphering maps with the aid of a magnifying glass, studying old records and diaries, I found the wonderful three-volume history of Pierce County by W. P. Bonney in our own library. They were the gift of Mrs. Eugene W. Cade in 1934 and no better history can be found. All the data I needed was there, corroborating what I had discovered in weeks of research.

Memories cannot always be depended upon for accuracy, but Mr. Bonney, descendant of one of the earliest pioneers, had verified his data from records and we can feel sure that he knew whereof he wrote.

He found that a married man could have 640 acres if taken before December 1, 1853, under the Oregon land law or donation land act passed September 27, 1850, under President Filmore. This was reduced soon to 320 acres which it was thought would cause a rush of immigrants to the Northwest. This did not take place because of the difficulties of the journey across the plains and over the mountains.

The British wanted the Columbia River to be the boundary but when the treaty was signed in 1846 placing the boundary where it remained, the Hudson's Bay men at Vancouver, Washington, had orders to induce settlers to go south of the Columbia. But the Yankees were stubborn and thought if the land toward the north was valuable for Great Britain it must be for the U. S. and they continued to make their way north.

In 1851, 58 claims were taken. In 1852 there were 117 and when the donation act expired in 1854 only 985 had been taken in all of Washington territory.

The pre-emption land act preceded the DLC act and had become a law in 1841. Under it a man could buy land without living on it. In 1850 this law was extended to include Washington territory. It did not become effective until 1862.

DL claims and pre-emptions were taken in the following districts in western Washington: Steilacoom, The Lakes, Nisqually River, The Muck, Clover Creek, White River and the Puyallup. They were taken near water courses or lakes or springs. Rivers were the source of navigation by canoe as there were no roads or bridges. These settlers laid the foundation for the remarkable growth of Pierce County. We will concern ourselves only with those claims taken out on the north side of the Puyallup River where Sumner was located.

After resting from the long journey, William M. Kincaid and his oldest son John F. came to the Puyallup by canoe up the Stuck River. They learned from the Indians to call it the Stuck as the Indians spoke of it in their gutteral sound as "Stuch um" meaning "big fish." Stuck was the nearest they could come to spelling it. Perhaps, as the river was a small stream then, often so low that it could be waded across, huge salmon came up it to spawn, hence the Indian name.

What a sight this forested valley must have been to men who had come over the dry, dusty plains of the midwest! They found the soil was rich humus from centuries of fallen vegetation. Tall cedar, fir and spruce trees promised a wealth of lumber.

As the government had not yet surveyed this new land, claims could be staked of any shape, taking in good land by the rivers. The measurement was by chains and links, the pioneer way of computation. A chain was 100 links or 66 feet.

Because Kincaid was a widower, his wife Nancy having died just before his coming west with his seven children, he could have only 160 acres. It does not seem fair when he had such a family. It was on his claim that Sumner was first platted. All claims adjoining his give his corners as their starting point. Abrial

Morrison took 320 acres just north of the Kincaid clain. Geroge Haywood got 326.49 acres northeast of Kincaid's. Jonathan W. McCarty took 320 acres west of the Stuck adjoining the Kincaid claim.

Isaac Woolery joined the Kincaid DLC running to the Puyallup River going west, taking in what is now Greenlawn opposite the R. S. More and R. Nix claims. His claim joined that of Willis Boatman.

When children of the Woolerys died he buried them where the Pioneer part of our cemetery is now and gave land for the cemetery telling all pioneers they could use it as a burying ground.

Abraham H. Woolery (Aunt Pop's husband) took 321.73 acres beginning at the Meade-McCumber Road and running to the Puyallup River south and joining L. F. Thompson on the west. Levant F. Thompson had taken a claim where Dupont is now but did not prove up on it and so lost his rights and came to the valley and bought a pre-emption claim given to him by the U. S. government signed by President Grant. All claims at this time were signed by him.

The claim of Willis Boatman was cut by the Puyallup River. When it was surveyed, it was decided to give him vacant land adjoining his claim omitting land on the south side of the river. This enlarged his acreage where North Puyallup is now located.

Jacob R. Meeker abandoned his claim he had taken on the prairie. November 25, 1854, he married Mrs. Nancy Burr, a widow who had come in the Kincaid train, and took a pre-emption cert. 4268 east of the Kincaid DLC. He died before receiving the patent which was issued to his widow and heirs. He was the father of Ezra Meeker, the hop king and trail blazer. Aaron Meeker and Melinda Meeker (Daniels) were their children and heirs of the parcel of land, the other heirs relinquishing all claim to it.

What memories these old abstracts with their records brought to my mind as I perused the history of people I once knew in the 1890s!

Adjoining the A. H. Woolery claim was Addison H. Perham who sold to Robert Grainger whose wife in 1904 bought the Isaac Lemon claim two miles east of Sumner. Perham had 159.60 acres and Lemon 161.18. George W. Sloan, a Presbyterian minister at Steilacoom, also a surveyor, surveyed these claims in 7872. The fractions show that the staking was irregular and when the claims were surveyed sometimes the acreage was over and sometimes under the 160 or 320 entitled to the settler. Van Tassell owned 300 acres at the foot of the hill where the Weber-Ritter slaughterhouse stands and included land up the hill. He bought it from my father. As a girl I lived there when my father leased the farm. His land touched the Peter Huber farm, now the Corliss place, went to Parker Road and east to the mill property.

Much fascinating history is contained in old abstracts, of weddings, deaths, mortgages, testimonies to character, redemption of mortgages, transactions, etc. Many a second marriage is recorded when a husband or wife had succumbed to the rigors of pioneer life; then families were united in a second wedding. Sherwood Bonney is a good example of this.

Sherwood and Timothy Bonney, brothers, started together for the west with their families, Sherwood having four children and Timothy three. At the Cascade Locks August 4, 1853, Timothy and his little daughter died. August 14 Sherwood's wife died also and all three were buried there.

Elizabeth (Mrs. Timothy) drove her team the rest of the way caring for the children of both families. What wonder that when they reached Steilacoom Sherwood and Elizabeth were married and later had five children. Mrs. Bonney was a wonderful woman and many pioneer women gave testimony to her kindness and help given when children were born and women had to help each other, often without the aid of a doctor. W. P. Bonney, the historian, was one of their children.

A humorous story was told by W. P. Bonney: "Hearing a commotion in the back yard, Elizabeth investigated and told her husband, 'Your children and my children are teasing our children.'"

It would take too long to tell of all the purchases of land from the original land claims, but here are a few of them: William H. Baker bought 110 acres north of the Jonathan W. McCarty claim; J. R. Dickinson bought from A. Morrison where the factory is now located; Dr. Fred Williams bought from Mr. Morrison, selling later to Herbert and Sydney Williams.

John F. Kincaid writes that he was a lad of 16 when his father took his claim. When the Hudson's Bay men, George D. Hayward, George Dean, Isaac and Abraham Woolery, Willis Boatman, John Carson, Thomas Owen, Abrial Morrison, Isaac Lemon, Adam Perham and Jonathan McCarty, came to the Puyallup there were no whites living there. They all moved from Steilacoom in canoes, clearing the land, building houses out of hewed and split logs, making their tables and chairs. The windows were no doubt of oiled paper or muslin. Later panes of glass could be bought at Steilacoom and brought by canoes. The chimneys were built of sticks and mud. Tin dishes had to do until their goods arrived, coming around the Horn, which took many months.

Books were scarce, many having only the Bible and dictionary. Their diet consisted of deer meat and dried fruit, with vegetables which they grew in the rich soil. There were no insects or diseases to fight. White men brought these with them and then spraying became necessary.

Quote from J. F. Kincaid:

> From our arrival we had a hard struggle to get the necessities of life: flour and groceries were shipped around the Horn. Flour was $50 per barrel. In 1854 father paid $80 per barrel for pork and $84 per bushel for

potatoes and everything in proportion. Wages were high, wood choppers getting $4 per day (!) Father got a carload of pikes and was paid 10 cents per running foot.

Neighbors were often 20 miles away and women were lonely. Many wished they had never come west. Indians lurking in the surrounding forest wondered at these strange white men who built houses planning to stay in one place. It seemed queer to them that these men claimed to own their land, even drove them away when they walked right into their houses. They knew nothing of locked doors. Didn't these white men trust each other?

By a stream an Indian would set up his tepee of poles tied together at the top, leaving a hole through which the smoke of the fire could escape. He covered the poles with bark or skins; the women wove mats of rushes for beds laid around the inside of the tent. They would smoke fish and hang it out to dry. After a while they would pull down the wigwams and move to another place, often right beside the house of the white interloper. In the Indian's mind this land was free, as free as the air. When driven away the Indian's education began, education which ended in disaster for the settler.

William M. Kincaid and his seven motherless children, Ruth, the oldest, being 16, moved into the cabin built by the Stuck River near where John, the oldest son, built his home later. (The John Kincaid house was razed in 1965.)

Jonathan C. McCarty, a bachelor, had taken his DLC right across the river. Is it any wonder that he fell in love with pretty Ruth? The river was no barrier to his courtship. In 1855 they decided to get married.

Sherwood Booney was the justice of peace, then living at Steilacoom. They sent for him and when he came he found his jurisdiction extended only to the Puyallup River as that was the boundary of Pierce County at that time.

Consternation struck the wedding party! It was too far and too difficult to send to Seattle for a minister or another justice. Ruth exclaimed, "I have it! Let's go over to Robert More's. He'll let us have the wedding there. I know he will."

So, in canoes, the party went across the river and the Mores were glad to have the ceremony performed in their home. It was the first wedding in Pierce County. All went back over the river to celebrate the wedding. Ruth continued to run across the river on a foot-log to help her sister Susannah with her care of the family.

Indians continued to appear and one day a friendly one brought news that hostile Indians had come across the mountains. This frightened the Kincaid family and all crossed the river, Susannah carrying her little brother Joe. They hid on the hill all night. The old father, finding it hard to cross on the log, had to be helped over. The next morning all went to Fort Steilacoom where they remained, not coming back to the valley to live until 1859. The men came and worked the land but left their families at the fort for safety. While there Ruth gave birth to her daughter, Clara McCarty, who was the first and only graduate of the Territorial University in 1876.

When the men returned to see what had happened, they found all the homes had been burned and the stock had been carried away. With true fortitude and faith in the future of this valley they began again to build cabins and make their furniture. Ruth only lived to be 44 years old but did see her daughter graduate from the university.

Susannah, the second Kincaid daughter, was 14 when they came west. An Indian "tyee" offered several Indian ponies in exchange for her because he liked her sparkling black eyes and vivacious manner. He wanted her for a squaw for his son. He believed he paid a great compliment which caused much merriment in the Kincaid family. We shall have much more to tell about Susannah in a later chapter of this story.

An account of the Indian raids of November 1855 and the burning of the Kincaid, Woolery and McCarty homes is given in *History of the Pacific Northwest*, 1889 Vol. 1 p. 546.

Ezra Meeker wrote of William M. Kincaid: "In character, in fine sensibility, in true righteousness, in upright dealings with his neighbors, in firmness to stand for what he believed to be right, he was the peer of any man I ever knew—he was pure gold." (Taken from Laura McCarty Cook notes.) William M. Kincaid and Ezra Meeker were the sole dissenters in a hung jury in the celebrated Leschi case at the close of the Indian war.

Some readers will be interested in what Jonathan McCarty wrote about Leschi's death.

> Despite statements appearing in the *Tacoma Ledger*, the writer believes, on the strength of the testimony, that the Indian was really captured by the volunteers and brought into Steilacoom. As to the fact of his subsequent trial for killing of A. B. Moses, his conviction and sentence to be hung, all are agreed, though some at the time disagreed, claiming that killing in wartime is not murder.
>
> A young lawyer took it upon himself to defeat the hanging of Leschi. He got a warrant for the sheriff and had him arrested on the plea that he had sold whiskey to the Indians, and so the day for the execution went by. The governor then appointed another day.
>
> William Mitchell of Olympia was deputized to do the hanging instead of the Pierce County sheriff. Mr. Mitchell, thinking to prevent trouble, for there had been some talk of taking the prisoner away from him, brought a guard with him from Olympia. He took Leschi about half a mile from Fort Steilacoom on the 19th day of February 1858 and hung the noted chief until he was dead, dead, dead . . .

Jonathan McCarty tells more in this account of his wife Ruth's hardships.

After leaving my claim in October 1858, times being dull, with little work to do where it was safe from Indians, I and my wife went to Oregon where I split rails taking cows for pay, near Eugene City. I split 20,000 rails, traded my cows for oxen and bought two ponies. In the fall of 1858 my wife and I mounted our ponies, she carrying her babe of 18 months. We drove our 10 oxen to Steilacoom where we sold them. It was a rough, hard trip for a woman. She was thrown from her horse three times on the way, either by getting into jellowjackets' nests or having her saddle turn. Fortunately neither she nor the baby were hurt." (!!! my exclamations.)

They returned to their claim near the Stuck River in 1859.
He continues:

An incident occurred in August which sounds amusing now, but might have been serious then. Some Indians turned their horses into my pasture without permissions. I ordered them out, they refused to leave. I seized one of them by his hair and applied my stogy boots pretty thoroughly. Soon the whole camp came running toward me with their knives and hatchets, crying 'Memaloose, memaloose' meaning 'to kill.' I grabbed a board about four feet long vigorously hammering five of them. They took their horses and left, my hired men standing by, not interfering. I reported to the Indian agent and he wrote me to whip them when they gave trouble. I afterwards hired Indians and they have given me good satisfaction.

He wrote this for the *Tacoma Ledger*.
From the *Seattle Post-Intelligencer* February 21, 1870, quote:

Mr. Wm. M. Kincaid of the Puyallup valley died a few days ago. He was quite an old man, seventy-five years or near that. He was a worthy and highly respected citizen, and an old settler in Pierce County.

Bancroft's *History of Washington, Idaho and Montana*, 1845-1889, page 36 says:

Wm. M. Kincaid was born in Lexington, Kentucky, settled in Washington with his four boys and three girls, having come in an immigrant train in 1853. He was driven out by the Indian war, but returned to lay the foundation for a town named Sumner.

In 1869 just prior to his death he sold 40 acres, his NE quarter, for $320 to Fred C. Seaman who had married his daughter Laura. This is the forty which Laura Seaman, after the death of her husband, sold to George H. Ryan who had come west in 1872, and acted as bookkeeper to the Pope and Talbot sawmill at Port Gamble. He heard about the rich Puyallup Valley and came down to look it over buying this 40 in 1873, for $1,000.

The town of Sumner got its name from a popular statesman of the last century, Charles Sumner, whose name was drawn from a hat in 1875.

The village first was known as Franklin, but since there was another by that title already in the Washington Territory, and since a post office was needed, a new name had to be chosen. Three of the town fathers decided to change it.

George Ryan wrote in some of his records of how he and L. F. Thompson met in Joe Kincaid's store and each put a name into a hat. A passing boy was asked to draw one and picked the slip with "Sumner" on it. When the town was incorporated in 1891, that is the name which went up on the railroad depot.

The remainder of the William M. Kincaid donation land claim was sold to his son John Francis for $1190. This was 119 acres. In 1877 John deeded to the trustees of the Presbyterian church a triangle described as we know it today, along the railroad from the depot to Main Street, thence to Traffic Street and back along Traffic to the depot.

In 1877, March 31, the trustees sold to George H. Ryan and George H. Everett the triangle bounded by the railroad from the depot to Main, from there just beyond where Zech's garage stood and back to the depot. Some of us can remember when the RR watertank stood by the track and the trains stopped while the pipe was swung from the tank to the engine and the thirsty engine filled. The section house stood there containing the handcar used by the workers to keep the track in repair. It was worked by hand. The young people who had little for entertainment used to borrow it to go to Puyallup and Mrs. Margaret Stewart Espy Bow had many a laugh about their fun on the handcar, in the early eighties.

On the rest of the triangle a skating rink was built which we will describe in another chapter.

In 1873 the Northern Pacific announced that Tacoma would be the terminus of their line. This delighted the settlers in the valley. When a branch ran through to Seattle, it RAN THROUGH WITHOUT STOPPING! The NP officials said they could not stop until a depot was erected and this they were not able to do at this time. Public-spirited Mr. Ryan built the depot at his own expense and paid the salary of the agent for a year. He was reimbursed later and the NP took over the station. This did much to stimulate the growth of the town.

John F. Kincaid married Nancy Wright, the daughter of Benjamin Wright, July 5, 1868. Israel Wright's daughter Rebecca was married to Robert Smith

More December 5, 1868. Israel and Benjamin were brothers; therefore these marriages linked the Kincaid and More families.

Wright's addition to Puyallup extending to Clark's Creek was part of the Wright DLC. Edith More Herr, the daughter of Robert and Rebecca, still lives on the original More DLC just beyond the Puyallup River. This family seemed part of Sumner but as there was no bridge the children went to Puyallup to school.

After John and Nancy Kincaid deeded the lot as a site for the Presbyterian church, the building was erected in 1877. Dr. George F. Whitworth had been preaching in the schoolhouse on Division Lane which is now Main Street. Once a month he rode out from Seattle on horseback, fording rivers, etc., never missing an appointment.

A union Sunday school had been started by John Avery and preaching services were held every Sunday, ministers from Steilacoom of different denominations filling the pulpit.

A minute in the record book of the Presbyterian Church gives the baptism in the schoolhouse of Laura, Estella and Edwin Meade Thompson by Dr. Whitworth February 13, 1876. These were the children of Levant F. and Susannah Thompson.

The schoolhouse was called Liberty schoolhouse. Mrs. E. Palmer Spinning taught in it at that time. I think she was Mrs. Ben Spinning, Ben being the brother of Dr. Charles H. Spinning, the pioneer doctor.

George H. Ryan bought another eleven acres north of Main Street from John Kincaid. A clause in the abstract shows what William M. Kincaid left as an inheritance to the town which he laid out. When all deeds were executed this clause is included. Don Zech's abstract contains it, but we will copy the one given to George H. Ryan when he bought the eleven acres.

This clause troubled some who owned part of this property and gradually heirs had to sign a release. Some did this very reluctantly, as the pioneers who went through hardships to gain their claims wanted to have the town a place fit for boys and girls to grow into good citizens, free from contaminating influences.

This is the clause:

> The aforesaid grant, conveyance and covenants are made upon the express condition and are so understood and accepted by the party of the second part that his heirs, executors, administrators and assigns shall not allow, suffer, or permit any intoxicating drink or drinks to be manufactured, made, distilled, stored, sold or given away upon said premises, nor any gambling to be carried on, nor any house or other place of immoral practices thereupon, and any violation of the above conditions

or either of them shall absolutely divest said party of the second part, his heirs, executors, administrators and assigns or the estate granted and the same shall ipso facto revert to and revest in the parties of the first part and their heirs and assigns, as fully and completely as if the aforesaid grant and covenants had never been made and all covenants of said parties of the first part shall thereupon cease and determine and the consideration paid.

CHAPTER 2
LIFE IN 1870s

An extract from a letter written May 3, 1878, by Lucy V. Ryan to her grandmother in Wisconsin follows telling about the little church built in the valley.

The other day, Mr. Whitworth called, for in a few days he was to leave for the east, going to Pittsburg to a great Presbyterian gathering. Twenty-six years since he came here as a Presbyterian minister and this is his first return. He is a smart man, middle-aged and resides in Seattle. He has preached in this valley once a month ever since I came four years ago.

Two weeks ago last Sabbath the new Presbyterian church was dedicated. He, Dr. Whitworth, had solicited the funds from its mostly in San Francisco and Portland. It is a very fine little church, Gothic, with modern improvements, such as stained glass windows and tinted walls. The pulpit is very handsome. It is of California laurel and ash and so is the orchestra. The woodwork Dame Nature wrought in such lovely hues and exquisite designs. It is only oiled. The tower is a fine piece of work. It is the handsomest church I ever saw, far too good for us hoodlums. It is set among the cedars and just a nice walk from our house; time to compose one's thoughts. Mr. Lindsley of Portland was the speaker at the dedication.

We might notice here that this pulpit stands in the executive parlor of the present Presbyterian church. The pews made in 1877 are in use in the Sunday school rooms and a man who knows, told us not long ago that antique furniture makers would pay a fancy price for the wood in these pews as it is very rare and that we must prize them. The marbletop communion table, given by Mrs. Susannah Thompson, and the two cane-seated walnut chairs are also in the sanctuary, bringing back sacred memories to old timers.

This is a good place to quote a letter written by Mrs. Ryan in the next year, 1879, to her grandmother, as it shows she was not a member of the Presbyterian church. Mrs. Lettie Williams (Boatman) told in her memoirs that the Christian church was meeting at their home in North Puyallup at this time. Mrs. Williams also told of camp meetings conducted in their grove and I remember George Stewart telling me that a man who worked for them walked all the way to the Boatman's to the Christian church rather than attend the little church in the valley, which George felt was rather foolish. Quote from Mrs. Ryan's letter, June 16, 1879:

> I know that your heart will be glad to hear that George and I were baptized and united with the Christian church. I will send you a Christian paper in this mail. One of the neighbors sent it to me. The editor is the founder of Christian College. He is now president. He attends the college during the day, preaches three times a week and edits this sheet during his evenings. He has a church in Monmouth of 200 members. He is a very intelligent man, a fine speaker, a man that preaches the TRUTH.

While not a pioneer, Mrs. Lucy V. Ryan demonstrated in her letters to her grandmother that she lived a pioneer life. George Ryan bought his 40 acres from Mrs. F. C. Seaman in 1873. He was engaged to Lucy in Wisconsin. She was eagerly waiting to join him in the new country.

Her grandmother, who had raised her, would not let her travel alone to San Francisco to be married but when they heard that a Mrs. Gray was going there they hurriedly made plans for Lucy to join her for the trip in 1875. This was quite a venture and her grandmother prayed daily that she would not be scalped by Indians.

The wedding took place May 10, 1875, in a cold hotel room in San Francisco, the bride wearing a dress she had had made for parties. It was wool merino, with bustle effect, long train, puffed sleeves and a tight basque. The couple came up by boat, the *Pacific*, on a stormy sea which made the bride seasick, but she was a courageous soul and unflinchingly bore with the hardships in spite of her tender upbringing.

In 1875 anyone who had to go by sea dreaded it. A minister, George Sloan, who had been preaching in the valley occasionally, wrote to William M. Kincaid a letter which depicts his misgivings:

> It is with reluctance that I embark on the bosom of the ocean to steer away from the place I love . . . 'The Golden Gate' on the Pacific is the vessel that is appointed to convey about 800 or 1,000 human beings over their dark waters. Pray for me my dear brethren . . . Now goodby but not forever, for swiftly will I turn toward the romantic land of Puget Sound, and bend forward while I run for fear the delay will be too protracted. Gov. Stevens and lady and family are all going on the Golden Gate.

The letter is the prized possession of the Misses Swezey, great granddaughters of William M. Kincaid. (Now in the Sumner Museum.)

When the ship docked at Old Tacoma, the bride took a room at the hotel, waiting for the real homecoming to the Puyallup valley. It was too muddy for wagons to get over the narrow roads to the Indian reservation. She would have to go to the reservation in a canoe.

She wrote to her grandmother:

> I can't say that I regret coming west, even though things are not as pleasant as I would like to have them.
>
> Sitting by the window is your girl looking out on the blue waters of the sound. What do I see? Little sailboats and big sailboats. A lovely spot this is. The hotel is built right over the water. It's a very large building, the lower part is a warehouse and the hotel is above. The dining room and water-closets are all above. Nearly all the rooms face the water. It's very noisy here as the boats discharge their freight right on the veranda, which always sets the hotel shivering when they come up against the wharf.
>
> On the other side of the building the train runs right up to it and stops because there the ties end. Cars run from here to Portland every day. O, the noise of the cars as they run the length of the building is deafening. It sounds so loud as it is over the water.

She heard of some furniture that she might be able to buy and this is the way she described her ride to the house where it was:

> Put on my water-proof and overshoes ready when the landlord chartered the wagon that brought in lumber, not even a board on it. He put a wet bag of hay on one of the rails and I got on and just hung—clung to my umbrella until a gust of wind turned it inside out and broke it. O, how it did rain! I never was out in such a storm. Where I wanted to go was half a mile up a steep hill."

She found when she got there that the furniture had been sold so she walked back to the hotel.

When the bride finally reached her future home, it was a cabin set in the midst of a forest. The reading room of the present library was part of the original house where they set up housekeeping. Neighbors were far away and she often told in later years of the kindness of the earlier settlers.

She said that when Mrs. Grainger rode out of the forest on her horse that she felt she had never seen a more beautiful sight. Mrs. Robert Grainger was a beautiful woman and they became fast friends. They used to revel in the beauty of the woods. Here is a description of its beauties:

I'll enclose a few sprigs of moss. You can't conceive of the variety and beauty of our mosses. Everything in the wintertime is draped, even the roofs of the houses are verdant with moss; brakes and licorice growing as finely as you please. Nothing is quite as lovely as the "air moss."

Tis exquisite in places, every tree and shrub is festooned with this airy substance. Once can imagine himself in fairyland, so light and nothing-like is this strange formation. It grows yards and yards long and is never still. I often think of the girls at home when I am in some wild weird spot, wishing they could enjoy it with me. Some of the ladies living here make collections of mosses, they are lovely. This I am enclosing is feather moss, put it in water and it will curl again. One spray grows on top of the other.

I can remember when Mrs. Grainger used to decorate our little church with mosses and ferns from the woods. I always thought she looked like a delicate piece of china as she worked with flowers and greenery. They lived east of Sumner.

Mrs. J. R. Dickenson was another good friend. Once when Lucy went to visit her she got lost coming back to her home and thought she heard a bear and ran through the woods coming out into a clearing where she saw a man standing in the doorway of his cabin smiling at her. She started to ask the way home when he asked, "Did you think you saw a bear?" and she saw it was her own husband and her own home. Another time she heard a hen cackle and went to find the nest and got lost again. She found herself at the Joe Kincaid home near where the NP depot is now.

Mrs. L. F. Thompson was another who was a tower of strength to the new bride, showing her how to make the best of pioneer life as Susannah had had much experience.

In 1876 her first child (Lucy V. Ryan's) was born and she went down to the reservation in a wagon, from there in a canoe to the dock at Old Tacoma and took the steamer Zepher to Seattle where my husband was born. She was called a "tenderfoot" because she wanted a good doctor's care.

When her next son Lewis was born she was in Sumner and then had the care of two babies for there was just 14 months between their ages.

While in bed with Lewis she wrote the following to her grandmother (February 25, 1877).

About the savages and scalps you ask after, they say there is no danger. You probably call for a reason. I'll give you the old settlers' reasons. In hoppicking we have parts of seven or eight tribes here. These tribes are not friendly with each other. Last fall we had the Klickitats and the Muckleshoots that would not speak. They were camped within call but were very hostile. They have to be united to attack the whites. Some tribes are very friendly to us and would fight for us. A better reason is, their wives and children are here. It would be impossible for them to cross the mountains in a single night as they would have to do after an attack.

There are but two passes through the mountains and they would be caught before they could get away. These 'scalpers' that come over are horsemen, do their fighting on horses, and this heavy timber country is no place for that kind of fighting. The salt water Indians are friendly. Rest assured we are all safe.

She didn't tell her grandmother that the settlers had all been armed by the government.

I suffered agonies last hoppicking. I was weak, in bed with my baby. Some foolish neighbors filled my head with fears. I could not sleep nights for Indians whooping and hollering. I fancied I heard warwhoops and groans. An old "yarb" doctor came in one day and yarned that we might all be scalped. I was ready to swallow everything. Mrs. Jones got up in wrath and called him out. She told him he was an old fool to talk that way before a sick woman. If we were anywhere but in this valley, we might look out for our top-knots. We are so near navigation, railroad and telegraph that it would be easy to call for help and the Indians know it. So don't worry for we are in no danger.

Her attempt to hold a claim up on the hill east of Sumner is a graphic account of her courage.

Two years later, May 1, 1879, she wrote about her troubles in proving a claim:

Two weeks ago, nothing would do but I should go and make proof on our "preemption." It joins the Averys' claim. The boys made me think someone would jump it if I didn't go. Avery had come down, and I was supposed to go back with him. We got a late start as I was not sure I should go.

Our "coach and four" consisted of a rack with boards for sides, held in place by two round sticks at the end. Two yoke of oxen who had not had a bite of grain all winter, and who had a fine display of ribs, were to draw us.

We piled in among the bundles and boxes and settled ourselves. I thought my seat a little warm and found I was sitting on the bread I had just taken from the oven. G. H. had dropped the light cream cake I had made when he was adjusting it into the load. These two incidents put a damper on our start. I had prepared our food with so much care. With a "whoa, haw and gee" we jogged along. Those we met cheered us by saying we would never get there.

I must tell you of the hill we climbed that is said to be 600 feet high. The ascent is very gradual but difficult with a load and poor oxen. On one side of the road is a deep canyon. No team could pass as the road is so narrow. When we reached the top we could see miles and miles of forest and plain. We could see Tacoma, the Cascades, and Olympic ranges all snowcapped. It was a magnificent sight, one an artist would rave over. The other hill went straight up. The boys and I walked up and puffed some, you better believe.

So far, all went lovely, but when within five miles of our destination, the rain came down with a steady patter. Night came on and the worst of our road yet to go over! MUD! MUD! MUD! You never saw such mud! I wonder how we ever got through. The last four miles was nothing but mud.

The water came into our wagon-box several times. The wheels were up to the hubs in mud. They would strike a root and stop; and the rain pounded down. The night was so black I could not see my hand before my face. The wind howled through the forest. O, I never want to experience another such a night.

Once we struck something, no go. Avery felt around and found we were stuck on a log and couldn't move. The oxen wouldn't back so over the log the wagon had to go. I was afraid we would upset, so he helped me out on the log. He woke the boys (remember, they were little, one was two and one was three!) and set them out on the log. Of course they howled. The rain was soaking us through. You better believe I was pretty blue out on that log! I was afraid we would have to stay out all night. Fate was kind; we got over and again we crawled along slowly. Avery exclaimed, "What would your grandmother say if she could see you now!" He was afraid the oxen would come to an everlasting whoa. He waded to his boot tops in mud because he had to keep at the head of his leaders.

Were we truly thankful when we reached our shanty! Avery's was a mile beyond. We could go no farther. I never was more glad to reach shelter than that night. It was like a palace to us, though the door was off its hinges and there was no light in the window.

I found my tallow candle and matches that were tucked in my lunch box. A great blessing lay piled in the corner in the shape of dry wood. Avery got a roarer going and I for the first time realized the value of light and heat. O, isn't it a comfort when caught in such a plight to have fire and light! The children's underclothing was dry but I was soaked to the skin. Avery was afraid I would be sick. I had brought a small mattress for the boys and had expected to get one for myself at Avery's.

We put our clothes to dry. I found an old tin pail and made strong tea which we drank. We had milk, bread, butter, jell and cold meat.

We kept a hot fire all night. I lay down on a pile of straw and felt good clear down to the tips of my toes as I tried to sleep. I was so thankful for the warmth and light.

Morning came and we, tired and cold got into our "coach and four" and rolled on to Avery's. There we had breakfast. When I came down with a horse team we had no adventures. The boys had colds but I was only stiff.

The next excerpt from her letters shows her fears that her boys will become heathen Chinese or uncouth Indians. They could speak the jargon called "pidgin English" which was a combination of the Chinese and Chinook. Because they had Indians and Chinese both working for them the settlers had to have a common language.

The Chinese cook, Chan, who helped with the housework said "Missee Lyan, new missie all light, she not muchee tall, not muchee fat; her eyes all same heap gold. She have halo cue and talk like Melican music."

Excerpt from another letter:

Harry has concluded to let a pig-tail grow and talk Chinese. He stays with them entirely. I am expecting him to throw away his spoon and eat with chop-sticks. I can't bear to have him so much with them but I have so much to do I can't chase him all the time. They feed him sweetmeats and they teach him to be saucy. They say, "He heap smart and like heap big boy."

Lucy and George Ryan had five children—Edith Ryan Van Vechten, Harry R., Lewis D., Charles A. and Warren W. Edith, the wife of Dr. Ward Van Vechten of Tacoma, is the only survivor. Lucy died in 1925 and George in 1934.

At the time of their mother's death, the Ryan children gave her home to the community of Sumner to be used as a library.

The old part of the house, built in 1875, was covered with English ivy, planted by Lucy. It had crept inside the building and hung in festoons within the walls.

The library was installed in the portion of the building dated to the 1880s. It grew so rapidly that more room was necessary. After consideration, the old section was restored in 1930.

Copy of letter written by Mrs. E. Palmer Spinning (Mrs. Ben) to Mrs. Lucy V. Ryan (Puyallup, February 20, 1911):

My dear Friend:

Your letter just received and read with pleasure. I enjoy so much receiving and answering letters, especially those coming from old true and tried friends, as I have always thought you to be.

In regard to the early history of Sumner, I will try to refresh my memory regarding the part I took in it.

I first came to this valley to teach a ten months' school, March 4th, 1872, in the new Liberty schoolhouse, here. There was no Puyallup then. The name of the post office was Franklin, don't remember who was postmaster. January 13, 1873 I taught school in Stuck, as district number eight, now Sumner, was then called.

Franklin post office then served both sides of the river. I think it was in 1876 that I took in the post office as Mr. McMillan refused to keep it longer and I kept it about two years. It was you who succeeded me as postmistress. I think I made about fifty dollars out of the post office. In regard to the post office going back to Mr. McMillan's store, I remember he said if it was sent there he would pitch it in the river. I think the post office was kept at the Vinings' when I first came to Puyallup by Mr. James Wright (Mrs. John Kincaid's brother) in the fall of 1872.

Now that we have the ballot we need a little coaching how to use it. Have you registered yet? Don't forget to do so or you will be sorry when the time comes to vote down the saloon etc.

Love and best wishes,
E. Palmer Spinning

CHAPTER 3
HOP BOOM

Several picturesque old hopkilns, patined by time, their wooden ventilators etched against the sky, stand as mute reminders of the cycle of prosperity which swept the Pacific Northwest, especially in the Puyallup valley, in the 1880s and then collapsed.

The settlers who had staked their claims were adjusting themselves to primitive pioneer living.

In Olympia Charles Wood, who operated a brewery, sent to England for some hop roots. The hop was a wild perennial vine in the nettle family, which ran riot in England and on the continent.

Yeast which was used to leaven bread and also to make beer was made out of the catkins which grew on this vine.

In 1865 Mr. Wood sent a bundle of roots to John Meeker, a school teacher at Steilacoom. John walked the 20 miles to Puyallup valley where his father, J. R. Meeker, lived on his preemption claim at Sumner. On the way he stopped at the cabin of his brother Ezra and gave him a few of the roots. Ezra claimed to be the first hop grower in the Northwest. By 1871 he had large fields of hops. The first year he harvested 185 pounds selling them at Olympia for 85 cents a pound.

As hops have very long roots, the virgin soil in the valley was ideal for the propagation of this plant. The fallen vegetation, moistened by the rains, had accumulated until the soil was very deep and rich.

The pioneers had visions of future wealth and went wild in anticipation. The forest echoed and re-echoed with the sound of ax and saw as the giant trees were laid low. In the prepared soil eight or 10 sets were planted in each hill. When they sprang up quickly only the strongest were left and how rapidly they grew, winding around the poles and curling among the wires strung between them.

By September the vines were loaded with fragrant hops. When they were ready for harvesting they dropped a yellow powder when crushed in the hand.

Then hordes of Indian pickers arrived, coming from Canada in canoes made from large tree trunks, and over the mountains on horseback. The Indians could not understand why the white men worked so hard. They let the women do most the picking while they sat and gambled with the money their wives earned.

By their tepees hung whole dried salmon, the Indian's favorite food. Children of the white settlers could never stand smoked and dried fish as they always remembered the smell in the Indian camps.

The valley resounded with the bedlam of pidgin English (the Chinook jargon) which was a combination of Indian, Chinese and English. It was the universal language for the whites and Indians alike "Kla-how-ya" (how are you?), "Klat-a-wa" (goodby or get out), "nika-halo-kum-tux wa-wa" (I do not understand your language) became the common greetings. Chinese pickers added their confusion of tongues when they were imported.

The hops were picked in large boxes having handles on each side. The poles were dropped into crotched sticks which held the vines out of the dirt.

The nights were made hideous by the wailing and pounding to drive out evil spirits when anyone was sick. It kept up from dark until dawn. The Indians always camped north of what is now Main Street.

Gambling accompanied by the rattling of bones at the Potlatch also kept the pioneers awake. By the 1890s women and children of the settlers took over the work and quiet came to the valley as the Indians were not called in for pickers.

Few can recall how the women made mitts out of the long, black cotton stockings worn in that period. This was to keep their arms from being scratched by the prickly vines. The growers winked at a trick everyone used.

As the hops wilted so rapidly, the hops were gathered in boxes, barrels, even on sheets or tablecloths laid on the ground. When enough was picked to fill a box the hops were quickly heaped in and fluffed up and a loud shout rang out, "Hop box full!" The foreman came and paid a big silver dollar for each box.

My! That dollar was BIG! It really was larger then than now as it could buy so much more. One dollar was usually a day's wage.

By the time the box reached the dry-kiln it was not more than half full although the weight was still there. It was carried up the ramp and the hops dropped to the drying floor. Sulphur was used for a bleach and the valley air was suffocating with the heavy fumes.

After drying, the hops were baled and shipped to San Francisco, the grower usually going along with his crop. Many of our old settlers amassed fortunes as the hops had an average yield of 1600 pounds to the acre.

J. R. Dickenson sold his crop at 84 cents a pound, clearing $30,000 in one year. His daughter, Mrs. Marie Dickenson Taylor, living in Tacoma, told me so. He built a beautiful home by the river across from where our factory district is now. He sent to Italy for black marble of which he had eight fireplaces constructed. He went to San Francisco and bought the best furniture. It is a pity that this house was torn down a few years ago.

In reading the *Sumner Herald* of May 25, 1894, I found this item of historic interest:

This week came into our hands a copy of the old *Pioneer-Democrat* dated July 4, 1856. On its yellow pages are recorded many incidents of historic interest, among them graphic accounts of recent battles in the Indian war, then in progress; an eloquent appeal before the house of representatives by Hon. Joseph Lane of Oregon on a bill appropriation of $300,000 for the suppression of Indian hostilities in the territories of Washington and Oregon; a notice of church services under the pastorate of Rev. G. F. Whitworth, and most important of all the following notice with its accompanying words of admonition and congratulation, bringing to our view the early happy days of two of our most beloved and respected townspeople and pioneers:

MARRIED—July 1st in Thurston Co. by the Rev. J. F. Devore, Mr. L. F. Thompson to Miss Susan Kincaid both of Steilacoom, Pierce Co., Washington Ter.

Accompanying the above notice we acknowledge the receipt of a slice of the bridal loaf, for which the wedded pair will receive the thanks of the *Pioneer-Democrat*. Friend Fred, remember that you were a member of our first territorial legislature and that you voted "Aye" on the passage of the law REGULATING MARRIAGE! We hope that you may never desire that law be repealed and may never feel like voting "Nay" in conforming with the obligations which the marriage ceremony rites inculcate. A long, happy life Fred, to you and your fair bride. Adhere to the principles of democracy, and may your motto be "E PLURIBUS UNUM" and may they all follow in the footsteps of your teaching. Fred, to thee we say, "Love thy wife FIRST, after that be just and fear not; Let all the ends thou aimest at be thy country, thy God and Truth, etc."

Levant F. Thompson, the prominent young politician, a member of the first territorial legislature in 1854, married Susannah Kincaid in 1856. He had extensive hop-fields. He erected a manor house in which chandeliers surrounded by crystal prisms hung from ceiling rosettes. A mural of hops painted by an Italian artist was topped by moldings of real gold leaf. Mrs. Douka tells me that they found the gold leaf still under the cover of paint.

The Doukas love the old house with its porticos and imported black marble fireplaces with the ancient old trees standing guard in the yard. Mrs. Mirriel Huntington and Miss Adelle Huntington restored this old home to much of its original beauty when they lived there. I will tell more of its first mistress in a later chapter.

Mrs. Laura Kincaid Seaman was married to Elijah C. Meade after the death of her husband. Mr. Meade also grew hops and he erected the lovely home now owned by Mr. Burns, the principal of Maple Lawn school. Mrs. Meade brought her three daughters with her, Nellie Seaman (Bergmann), Carrie Seaman (Church), and Jessie Seaman (Fox).

Later she and Mr. Meade had two charming daughters, Edith (Doll) Meade (Martin) and Sue Meade (Anderson). After Mrs. Meade's death Mr. Meade went to Alaska where he died. Those of us who attended the little old Presbyterian church in the 1890s will always remember him sitting on the front seat at every service. At one time he was the only elder in the congregation.

The Meade home went to Mr. and Mrs. Paulhamus, who had four children: Alice, a lovely child; Clay, Dwight and Caroline who lives in Seattle.

Dr. Joseph Clark from Pittsburgh and later his brother, Dr. Albert, were the next owners of this beautiful home with its attractive grounds, living there until selling to Mr. Burns.

George H. Ryan added what the family called the "new part" during the hop boom and Sydney Williams built his home north of town. Herbert, his brother, built what for years was one of the show places in Sumner, adjoining Sydney's. The fountain in front and the porticos gave it a beauty very unusual at that time. (Few houses built today have the grace and beauty of the old homes, everything is geared to practical use and work-saving plans. Who can say which is better? Not I.) Mr. Ames from Boston built the C. R. Lantz home about the same time. Neither of these men made his money in hops. Mr. Parker's home was across from the Ames'.

John Kincaid writes that he laid out the town of Sumner on his land after the R R came through.

In the meantime men, becoming rich through the hop industry, plunged too heavily as the price went up to over a dollar a pound. Members of the WCTU felt ashamed when they thought their better homes might be due to what they considered wrong if hops were used in the making of beer.

Then the bubble burst! Lice appeared simultaneously in every field, the vines becoming furry with the aphids. Panic struck the growers! Ezra Meeker sent his son to England to find a remedy for the scourge. Charles Hood, in Puyallup, invented a spray pump which could be drawn on a sled between the hop rows. A spray was brewed of quassia chips and whaleoil soap and shot on the insects from the spray pump. Barrels were hauled up and down the rows as the men worked tirelessly from dawn to dark trying to save their crops. It was all to no avail.

Because mortgages hung heavily on most of the beautiful homes they passed one by one into other hands, though many years went by before some of them were lost. The men who had other interests were able to keep them until their families were raised, and some paid off their mortgages as the old abstracts show.

God had something far better for Sumner than hop growing as our dairies and bulb and berry farms have proved. Dare I ask, what does the future hold for the once-rich soil of our valley, covered by paved freeways and housing projects? Will we have any room left for growing food? I wonder! Cycles pass, changes come and we who remember the past think long thoughts . . .

At that time houses were being built and neighbors were in walking distance. We mentioned that Kate Spinning, Ben's daughter, had married Joe Kincaid, and I must tell you something about her. She was highly esteemed by the men who went hunting, because she always cleaned the game for them. As the water had to be carried from the river that was a monumental task. She was a merry-hearted woman, always making the best of everything. Dr. Corliss told one of her babies, that it was the only child he ever saw laughed into the world. The bed broke down and she held the head up laughing all the time the baby was born. He said she could always see the funny side of anything. What courage!

OLD HOP KILN - NEAR SUMNER WASHINGTON —

CHAPTER 4
WHITWORTH COLLEGE BEGINS

Few people living in Sumner today realize that Sumner was once a college town, that Whitworth College, now sixth in size of the Presbyterian colleges in the United States, had its beginning in Sumner.

Someone may have wondered why a street is named Academy. In 1890 when the college was moved in to its pretentious building, the whole block bounded by Alder on the east, Cherry on the west, Academy on the north and College (now Park Avenue) on the south, was the college campus. One could scarcely call it by that name for it was a field where the two horses and the college cow kept it mowed. The *Sumner Herald* has an interesting article in 1892 asking that something be done about the college grounds—that they were a disgrace to the town.

No one in Sumner in those days had well-kept lawns and Cherry Street was one of the most beautiful streets in Sumner. The cherry trees almost met across the road, for after all it was just a road, though wooden sidewalks were built on each side.

When the Thompsons gave the land for a park and the name was changed from College to Park, it left the impression that Whitworth was just an academy. Even today that is what some may think. But though Whitworth began as an Academy in the little old Presbyterian church in 1883, when the Rev. George McKinley came as pastor, in 1890 when the Rev. D. M. Davenport came to the pastorate he asked Dr. Whitworth to see if the academy could be raised to the status of a college. As Dr. Whitworth helped in its beginning when the Rev. McKinley asked him, so again he went to the Presbyterian General Assembly and secured the means to erect the beautiful college building.

This building contained on the first floor the chapel seating 125 students, the living quarters for the faculty, the dining room, the kitchen, the music rooms and the library.

The second floor had rooms for the girl students and the dean of women and two recitation rooms. The third floor had 16 rooms for the men. Pictures of this beautiful college building with its porticos and dormers are to be seen at the library.

This liberal arts college had grown from the 13 academy students to about 100 enrollment. The names of the first ones who sat at improvised desks in the little pioneer church were Margaret and Charley Stewart, Nell Seaman, Stella Thompson, Linda Meeker, Luella Kincaid, Ella and Oro Oliver, Jennie and Lizzie Dickenson, Newell Wilson, Arthur and Ross McKinley.

When it became a college, students came from as far away as California, Oregon, Olympia, Ilwaco, Seattle, Carbonado, Wilkeson, and even from Alaska. Hal Gould and Archie Cameron, who lives in Puyallup, were two that came down from Alaska. Hal was a great athlete.

Whitworth's catalogue of 1892 gives the following:

The moral tone of Sumner has a reputation above that of any city or town on the Pacific coast. It is free from saloon influences and is surrounded by a very intelligent, active and enterprising people.

The male and female students will occupy separate wings of the building and no access permitted from one to the other. Miss Edmiston, a highly-cultivated and experienced teacher, will have exclusive charge of the young women, and will accompany them when necessarily called to leave the college grounds.

The young men will be under the care and supervision of the faculty while in their rooms and they will not be permitted to leave the college grounds without first obtaining consent.

The college athletic club is a member of the Western Washington Inter-collegiate Athletic Association. Out of 13 prizes given for first honors in the various contests, seven were won by the Whitworth team in Seattle May 13, 1893. They brought home the Spaulding trophy from the field meet.

In the field day of the WWAA held in Tacoma May 12, 1894, the championship trophy was again won by Whitworth, winning nine out of a possible 14 medals.

Every Sunday morning a familiar sight was Miss Edmiston filing into church with her girls, occupying two pews. This was compulsory. During the week she could be seen walking the country roads with her charges.

The young men were under supervision of the faculty but many amusing stories are remembered of their pranks. Instead of "panty-raids" they staged "pantry-raids." One night they were gathered in one of the rooms when footsteps were heard approaching. Professor Fox was on the alert. Quickly Frank Blackburn grabbed a piece of soap and began to froth at the mouth, lying flat on the floor. The boys said "Frank is having one of his fits." The professor quietly said "Come on Frank, let's go down stairs and talk this over."

Another story is told with many a chuckle by Dr. Van Vechten, a member of the second graduating class, now living in Tacoma. He lived on College Street right across from the college building. A wire had been strung between the southwest corner of the third story to the VanVechten house. Extra eats had often been swung across this wire to the hungry boys, for midnight feeds. Halloween was prank-playing time so the boys took the crockery used for toilet purposes (there was no indoor plumbing) and slipped them out on the wire. Great was the consternation the next morning when faculty members saw this exhibition. Professor Fox took his shotgun and shot down the "white owls" and the handles dangled from the wire for months.

Another Halloween prank was to block Main Street with outhouses hauled in by these boys. Their arrest followed the next day and when brought before the justice of peace, Mr. Guffy, he let them off if they would return the houses to their respective locations. Then they put Mr. Guffy in the cart and hauled him up and down shouting, "Rah for Guffy, he's our man, try to beat him if you can."

Another year they took wagons apart and carried them up on top of the store buildings where they reassembled them. That time they were required to take them apart and bring them down and return them to their owners. These boys were not vandals or delinquents but they tried the patience of the faculty.

During the 1890s the college found it hard sledding. There were less than 100 students and a large percentage were from the local area. They paid their tuition which was $12 a semester with pounds of butter, dozens of eggs, bales of hay and wood and coal. When this was not forthcoming some were told to keep on coming as it cost the college nothing to have them in attendance, and they were valuable students.

Some walked from Puyallup, some rode horseback, and some came on the train every day, as that was the only means of transportation. The girl day students wore calico dresses and thought nothing of it as they wanted the privilege of an education. The professors had little coming in for salaries.

Several of the girls took the teachers' examination and received certificates to teach and found schools. An amusing article appeared in the *Sumner Herald* which said one of the young ladies held a high position as teacher. When she called the editor on it, he said, "Well, your school is up on a high hill isn't it?" I was that teacher and the school was the old Kelly schoolhouse in 1897. Of course they were trying to show what Whitworth had done for its young people!

The Synod of Washington decided to move the college to Tacama when J. C. Armour made them a gift of $50,000 to give it stimulus. Whitworth went very well for a few years but again it was moved to Spokane in 1913 where it was located on the beautiful J. P. Graves estate. Now it is one of the leading church-related small colleges in the United States.

When Whitworth was moved to Tacoma, the property was bought by Mr. and Mrs. Bray. There were two houses on the property, at the corner of Alder and Academy, one owned by I. T. Darr and the other by the Gow family. Dwire Garrett lived for years in the Gow house and the Darr house was enlarged and made over by Dr. Mitchell into a hospital, in the 20s. Mrs. Elm lived there until a few years ago and now it has been torn down.

The Brays had housekeeping rooms in the old Whitworth building. Barbara Boss lived with them 13 years and when the Bryants came to Sumner they lived in it until they bought their home on west Main. The Penningtons also had rooms there until they moved southwest of town and the Masters family made it their home. All the Christian preachers made the Bray's home a stopping place. Mrs. Bray was an artist and painted lovely landscape scenes and flowers. She had her studio upstairs.

There are some living in Sumner who went to first grade there after the Brays moved out, when an overflow was needed. A fire in 1909 damaged the building and another in 1918 finished it so it had to be torn down. The Brays platted the land and sold lots for residences. The first edifice to rise on the grounds was the Catholic church.

CHAPTER 5
TEMPERANCE ISSUE

The observance of the 80th anniversary of the organization of the Woman's Christian Temperance Union, February 4 brings to mind the battles that were waged in the 1890s in the effort to keep Sumner free from saloons. The *Sumner Herald* issues have many interesting items which I shall quote for the sake of memory. Quote August 15, 1890:

> The 'drys' are waiting and watching. They are aware that their chances are not good for carrying this precinct, yet like Abraham they have faith and faith, we are told. In justice to them we must admit they have increased in number this past year.
> There are some though like the old Kentuckian, who voted for the man who had a whiskey barrel open at both ends.
> Very little is heard here these times about woman's suffrage while at this time last year the very atmosphere was full of it and petitions longer than rake handles were being signed to advance the interests of the cause.

In the October 24, 1890 issue there appears an item showing that a town meeting was called to try to remove the restricting clause which we included in our column December 12, 1963. This prohibited the sale of liquor on any property deeded by the Kincaids. A committee was appointed to confer with Dr. Whitworth, chairman of the trustees of Whitworth College, to see if he would try to get that clause removed from the property in that section of the town. The committee consisted of Henry Williams, J. R. Darr and L. R. Coombs. When they waited upon Dr. Whitworth he consented to do his best to get the restriction removed. Quote:

> This restriction is a mill-stone long on the neck of progression in this place. It is not in harmony with civil liberty or the American form of government. Its removal will stimulate business, etc.

It seems that they succeeded as December 12, 1890, there was published the strangest letter from the Rev. D. M. Davenport, pastor of the Presbyterian Church. It follows, quote:

Rev. D. M. Davenport,
    Dear Sir,
    We the citizens of Sumner wish you to be present at the opening of our new saloon. We want you to preach a sermon from the text Jeremiah 25:27.

They meant this part of that verse, "Thus saith the Lord of hosts, the God of Israel: Drink ye, and be drunken." But they failed to take in the rest of it as follows "and spue, and fall, and rise no more, because of the sword which I will send among you."
Reverend Davenport withheld the name of the signer but the letter closed promising he would be paid for his services.
This is the minister's reply:

You will allow me to reply through the column of your paper that I will be most happy to accept this invitation and will preach from the text assigned and my services will be entirely free. Give me the time for your grand opening, provide accommodation for at least 500 people, give me one hour and a half and we will insure you one of the most interesting occasions ever witnessed in the line of a saloon opening.
    I am your humble servant, D. M. Davenport.

He preceded this by saying he thinks the writer was an ardent supporter of saloons. He could not understand the object in having such an opening of a saloon. He said:

Perhaps they will have a mourners bench for those who fought the saloon in every legal way as long as they were property owners. Yet the ink was scarcely dry from signing pledges to keep the saloon out of Sumner until others began to plot to bring one in. Perhaps the writer wants the school children just a few feet away from this saloon to see a delightful object lesson.

He couldn't interpret the reasons for the invitation.
Reverend Davenport was a fisherman, a hunter and a sports lover and mingled with all trying to influence them for good and that may have had something to do with the invitation. But search as I did in following papers I could not find that he ever gave his sermon. I believe that his request frightened them. I would have liked to have heard that sermon for he no doubt would have used the context and given a hard-hitting message.

For sometime there had been agitation in the town for incorporation. Some favored it others opposed because they thought the taxes would be higher. The neighboring town of Kent was incorporated and the *Herald* had an article stating in its issue January 19, 1891, that thousands of dollars, nay hundreds of thousands of dollars, had been benefited at a cost of only $2,000 per annum. Besides Kent now had electricity! The editor urged everyone to vote the next Tuesday for incorporation.

The following is another interesting item from the *Herald*: "Name an unincorporated town that ever prospered and we will name the 8th wonder of the world."

In the same issue showing that the "wets" and "drys" were working hard over the matter of electing the right councilmen if the town did incorporate, quote:

> There are in the town of Sumner two factions of but one idea each. The only idea of one faction is that a town council should be chosen which would direct all its legislation in favor of saloons. The other faction is of the opinion that a council should direct all its legislation against saloons. Both factions are extremists and it is pleasing to see that neither has a large following.
>
> The men nominated for councilmen at the citizens meeting Monday night belong to neither faction and neither can dictate the policy of the council. A man of but one idea should never be called to fill a public office. Vote the ticket straight as nominated Monday night.

Now let us read of this meeting to vote on the incorporation and the nomination of councilmen.

Women did not have the right to vote and how they did talk to their husbands about the issues coming up.

A town meeting was called and that night the roads (one could not call them streets) were lighted by lanterns carried by the earnest citizens as they trudged past the livery stable and the blacksmith shop

There they had been congregating, discussing the matter of incorporation and who should be nominated for councilmen and mayor.

The clop, clop of horses hoofs was heard and the men arguing as they tied their horses to the hitching racks near the hall. Quote from the *Herald* issue of January 30, 1891, the results of the meeting:

> Headlines! "WE ARE THE PEOPLE!"
> The incorporation election was a walkover. The antis were not in it!
> A heavy vote was polled and the People's ticket elected without opposition. A spirit of enterprise pervades the citizens of Sumner.

Tuesday was a red-letter day for Sumner, a day long needed came at last and got here with both feet. A dark, dreary rainy day—rained from morning until night. Ohio people would call it regular Democrat weather. Didn't dampen the ardor of the voters who know a good thing when they see it.

Polls opened at nine with Henry Williams inspector, M. L. Cagley and L.R. Coombs judges; A. M. Rousseau and J. J. Coy, clerks.

Voters came quietly, voted and went out. No open electioneering was done near the polls, but friends of the incorporation worked hard on the streets and around the stores. Polls closed at seven and in two hours the results were made known as follows:

    For incorporation 110
    Against incorporation 21
            Majority 89
    For incorporation 2
    For treasurer, J. R. Biggar . . . 109
    Councilmen:
            John R. Darr 115
            Geo. E. Henton 102
            Wm. R. Lindsay 104
            Thos. Maloney 110
            Wm. L. Thompson . . 117
            Scattering 2

Sumner at last legally and unrevocably incorporated causes great rejoicing. Also a set of officers of judgment, ability and discretion.

When the results were made known the Sumner band of which Councilman J. R. Darr is the accomplished leader serenaded a few of the newly elected officers. Mayor Ryan and Wm. R. Lindsay each did the proper thing by bringing out boxes of fine cigars so until a late hour Havana smoke hovered over the town like a nimbus cloud over a camp meeting ground.

March 6, 1891, gives an account of the first meeting of the newly-elected "neutral" council, the incorporation having been legally established. We quote from the issue of the Herald of April 24, 1891:

There was an extended argument over how to enforce the ordinance which had been passed March 20. This ordinance had been given its first reading, regulating the sale of intoxicating liquors. It was decided to require $1,000 per annum for a license, this to be paid semi-annually in advance.

In the same issue, quote:

The contract for a 'lock-up' to be built on the lot purchased from G. H. Ryan near the depot was given to D. M. McMillan and the marshal instructed to build a fence around it.

Some of us remember the little "jail" never needed before in Sumner and how we looked at it askance when we took the train to Tacoma.

June 19, 1891, quote:

A petition from James W. McGrew was presented to the council for the privilege of conducting a saloon; also a bond was presented as required. The petition was granted and the clerk ordered to issue the license.

I might interject here that Bert Purvis told me that his mother had come to visit the Williamson Stewarts in the 1880s and when told that Sumner had no saloon while Slaughter had six, she decided to locate in Sumner. Thus Sumner gained a very fine family who contributed much to Sumner in the early days and who still do. He tells me many families came for the same reason. I believe the Horner family was one, also the Browns. All these families had boys and their mothers were ardent supporters of the temperance movement.

The reports of council meetings are interesting reading. Long articles on temperance were given regularly, and the meetings of the WCTU were given much space.

The fight went on over the saloon into the 1900s. "Wet" and "Dry" caucuses were held before every election. One time at the polls the women stayed near the entrance to have influence on the voters. A box marked "Wet" and one marked "Dry" received the votes cast. One man became confused because some relatives were standing by and when a "Wet" vote was discovered in the "Dry" box it was attributed to this voter. The "Drys" won and E. T. Guptil was elected mayor in 1903.

A Good Templars Lodge was organized July 5, 1895, with 15 members. G. L. Landin (Methodist minister), L. L. Benbow, school superintendent, Inez Guthrie, Mrs. Benbow, Joseph Stewart, George Myers and Clifford Everett were officers elected.

I was in the Loyal Temperance Legion and how we did work, trying to get everyone to sign a pledge. This read, "I will abstain from drinking cider, beer, wine or any alcoholic liquor." We took it seriously and when I was teaching in Sumner I attended a party at the McCarty's across the river. Dr. Boyd was pastor of the Presbyterian church and sat by me when they served cider and doughnuts. I would not drink the cider though it had been made that day! Poor Dr. Boyd out of courtesy to me had to leave his too. I was so in earnest because of my early training, taking part in Demorest contests, speaking on "The Voice From the Poorhouse," when I won my silver medal, and on "The Bible and the Liquor Traffic," when I won my gold medal. Professor Fox of Whitworth College helped me with the latter recitation and he said he couldn't see why I ever chose such a selection. But it was good, "Woe unto them that justify the wicked for reward and take away the righteousness of the righteous from him," etc.

We sang "Down with whiskey, vote it down, death to old King Alcohol, vote it down," etc. "We won't give up any more, we'll fight till the cause is won," etc.

I wish children today were taught the seriousness of the drink habit, as we were. We are told that prohibition caused more liquor drinking! That makes me remember a story that is true. When Sumner had no saloons a man had a still up on what was called "Ryan's Hill." When he went up there he found bears had gotten into the still and demolished it and were dancing around having an hilarious time.

James McGrew and Charles Fellender did have a saloon for a time but they did not last too long. In the August 30, 1895, *Herald* we read

> The New York Woman's Committee organized to oppose woman's suffrage says it would be an imposition upon women to give them the unwelcome and unsuitable responsibility of the ballot!

But one by one the states gave women the right to vote and this changed many attitudes on vital questions for the welfare and the education of children as well as adults.

Some of the women who fought against saloons in Sumner were the mesdames Patch, E. J. Stewart, Horner, Ryan, Burr, Fanny Meeker, Langdon, Bock, Beckman and the ardent worker of later days Artemisia Andrews, beloved editor of the *News-Index* from 1915 to 1948. No one ever lived who was a more staunch supporter of the WCTU.

Quote from the Buckley Banner in the Heralnd, 1904: "Sumner has gone dry again. They must like it." Shows that the fight continued into the 1900s. January 18, 1907, "Wets" won election.

February 22, 1907, council meeting. Ordinance 132 passed requiring $1,000 fee for running a saloon. License granted if it was closed from 12 to 5 a.m. each night. Sunday the same hours. No paint was allowed on windows, no curtains, no screens or blinds; no seats for lounging, no screen or fence allowed to hide the back door, and no high windows—must be left so anyone can see inside the saloon.

CHAPTER 6
HARDSHIPS OF PIONEER WOMEN

As one who knew personally many of the brave women who did without necessities, not to say conveniences, dared dangers and endured hardships to come with their husbands to make history and save our great Pacific Northwest for the United States, I want to bear tribute to a few more of them. Men pioneers are praised aplenty but few writers mention their wives, most of whom died young because of the rigors of pioneer life.

While the Mores lived across the river from what is now Sumner, in the early days they were a real part of the community life. They could only communicate with their friends on this side by crossing the Puyallup River in a canoe.

Edith More Herr, living on a part of the original DLC taken by her grandfather, Robert More, tells many thrilling tales of her grandmother's life in the early days.

Elizabeth Smith More was born in Scotland, the daughter of an earl. Her family disinherited her when she married a commoner. She was born in 1825 and died in 1884. When approached by an emissary from Scotland to return and claim her title, she replied, "No, I like the United States too well."

While on an errand of mercy, helping a neighbor to have her baby, her own little child pulled the tablecloth off the table, upsetting the lamp or candle causing the home to burn down. The father tried every means available to bring the child back to consciousness with no success.

Elizabeth used to help her husband with the farm work and fell from the top of a load of hay, fracturing her skull. The injury was slight, but eventually caused her death. If she had been living today, such conditions could be remedied by our physicians.

One of her pleasures was to cross the Puyallup to visit Mrs. Ghiradella whose husband had purchased land from Isaac Woolery. The men had contrived a way to pull the boat over the river with ropes and pulleys. How the needles clacked and tongues flew as these friends enjoyed visiting.

Elizabeth was very proud when Governor Stevens came for supper that she had a white tablecloth. It was the only one in the neighborhood and it was made of flour sacks fringed all around.

She watched the Northern Pacific Railroad being built and other changes come to the valley. Her life story would fill a book.

MRS. MARY ANN BOATMAN

Essie Williams Weisner has a diary kept by her grandfather, Willis Boatman, in 1853. She also owns part of his original donation claim at North Puyallup. Her mother, Lettie Boatman Williams, often told of the pioneer experiences of her mother, Mary Ann Boatman.

Mary Ann was just 18 when she came to the Pacific Northwest with her husband, Willis. In his diary he described the trip as very difficult. A broken tooth caused Mary Ann's mouth to swell so tightly that she could not open it for him to make the extraction. This made her very ill and at the same time he took sick and thought he was going to die. He advised her to sell the wagon and get back to her people. But they both got better and went on down the Columbia from The Dalles to Portland.

When they arrived, the only house they could find was a shed with a dirt floor and no windows. "Perhaps you think," he wrote, "that we had a good night's sleep, the first night under a roof in seven months. We did not, for we realized our situation, far from home, no money and in dire poverty."

He left her there and went up to Ft. Steilacoom where he found work and brought his family north. They finally settled on his claim at North Puyallup. Indians stole her three-year-old son John. Everyone in the valley and all the men from Steilacoom searched for the child. He was found hiding in a bush having escaped his captors. When they tried to wrap him in a blanket he screamed in terror, making them surmise that he had been carried away in a blanket.

Their other son was working in the hops as a young man and fell off the platform from which the hops were dropped into the kiln. He was paralyzed for seven years. He was engaged to be married and his fiance was faithful to him as long as he lived. People used to take him books and magazines and have discussions with him about articles he read. He was a very intelligent young man. This was all very hard on his mother. She was a very hospitable woman. Old pioneers have precious memories of dinners at her home. She was adept at carding and spinning cloth for their use. She was a great inspiration to the younger women of the 70s as she could always be relied upon for help when they needed it.

MRS. SUSANNAH KINCAID THOMPSON

I have told of the marriage of Susannah to Levant F. Thompson and of his building a beautiful home for her. Now I want to tell some of her experiences in the home which have been told me by her granddaughter, Hazel Thompson.

She was an immaculate housekeeper and each spring every room had to be thoroughly cleaned, the carpets taken out and beaten. These carpets were wall to wall and tacked down over straw and papers. The whole house was upset.

The men of the househould had to beat the carpets. Finally Levant rebelled. Said he, "If you will do just one room at a time we will beat the carpet. But no beating if you tear up the entire house. There is no place to sit; we are cold with all the windows open at once!"

She also had to content with many pets. The men brought home a fawn they had found standing beside its dead mother. It became a house pet, bounding in every time the door was open. One Thanksgiving day the table was all set and someone opened the window and in leaped the fawn right in the middle of the table. That was enough, the fawn was given to a zoo.

Then Mr. T. brought home a pair of monkeys. They would sit on his shoulder and scratch his head. One day they spoiled the family wash hanging on the line. They, too, had to go to the zoo.

Susannah and her daughter Stella went to Portland in the 1880s and while there ordered a clock from Paris. In those days everything worthwhile was imported. Mr. T. was provoked when they told him about it. When it came to his surprise it was a lovely Seth Thomas grandfather clock. Their granddaughter Hazel Thompson, living in Seattle, owns this clock which keeps perfect time and is valued highly.

Susannah was very kind to the young brides who came West unprepared for primitive living. They learned from her how to cook and to meet emergencies. They loved her dearly.

She was a charter member of the Presbyterian Church dedicated in 1878, teaching in Sunday school and participating in all other activities. The townspeople could set their clocks Sunday morning by her white horse at the hitching rack. She did not tie it, just laid the reins over it and as the horse grew hungry he ate his way along until she would find him several blocks away when she came out.

She was a wonderful woman, her influence is still felt in Sumner. The principles of her family did much to mold Sumner's early standards.

Quote from *Sumner Herald* February 7, 1890:

> Sumner's senator writes: In the *Seattle Daily Press* appeared a two column article from the versatile pen of Hon. L. F. Thompson, of his place, the only member of the present legislature who was also a member of the first territorial legislature. Mr. Thompson's letter is a very readable one. He aptly contrasts the appearance of this country as it was in the early fifties with what it is at the present. After an interesting account of the first territorial legislature he closes his article as follows:
>
> As a whole the first legislature was an earnest intelligent body of men who did. their work conscientiously and well. They had met in a wilderness, as it were, to carve out a new territory in the hope that it would

before many years be a state. They represented the untiring and dauntless spirit of the pioneers who have carried civilization and progress to the farthest bounds of our great national domain.

They were from the ranks of the adventurous and hardy men who came to carve out a new empire from the boundless virgin forests of the Pacific Northwest. They went about their work with energy and devotion to the public interests, and they built the foundation of the structure which is now the state of Washington, with a large measure of wisdom. In their intercourse with one another there was a hearty cordiality that made them warm friends, and after all these years it is a rare pleasure to let the memory linger over the pleasant scenes and incidents of that old time, and to recall the features and words of these old pioneers in legislation.

The first legislature of the state is now entering its end. Here, again, amid the same grand and beautiful natural surroundings, with the same kind faces of old still here to beam a welcome, it has been a pleasant duty to assist in a humble way the shaping of the legislature. It is well to find here the young men who have come up to manhood in our midst or have come from distant states to make their homes with us.

It is well, also, to find here some of the graybeards who are rounding out their lives of devotion to the development of Washington. Once more have ties of friendship been formed, and admiration been excited by the display of patriotic ability in the performance of the task to be done.

Henceforth, the memory of the old will be mingled with the remembrance of the new. One, the pioneer in clearing the path to progress, the other the pioneer in clearing the path to progress, the other the pioneer in the second great epoch in material development. Both animated by the sincerest desire to be right and to do good, each worthy of the other.

LEVANT F. THOMPSON

(Our park was given by the Thompsons and Thompson Street is named for them. The family had a great influence on the founding of Sumner.)

Gladys Lane Gray (Mrs. Paul) living on part of the original Lane donation grant has happy memories of stories told to her by her grandmother, of the strenuous trip west when she was just seven years old.

The Whitesells and Lanes settled where Orting is now located. William Lane married Elizabeth Whitesell, Mrs. Gray's grandmother. Elizabeth was one of seven children. Her mother cooked for three families on the trek west, with a baby in arms. She was a little woman not over 100 pounds but full of determination and energy. It was said that she walked all the way from Wisconsin to Washington. She and the children went ahead of the train picking spears of grass to feed to the hungry oxen and gathered buffalo chips on the plains to use for fuel.

Elizabeth inherited many of her mother's characteristics. She was an earnest Christian and entertained every itinerant minister who came to hold services in the valley. Mrs. Lucy V. Ryan wrote to her grandmother in Wisconsin that she and her husband went across the river in 1878 to hear the Rev. George F. Whitworth preach in the Lane neighborhood, probably in the Lane home. He preached there once a month when he rode out from Seattle.

Let us take a peep into the past and see how these women lived, how they did their work, and see some of the trials and hardships of housekeeping, raising a family, obtaining clothing when life was primitive in this valley.

We call them heroines. What is a heroine? Is it not one who lives steadily, sturdily and cheerfully day by day, developing a strong character and transmitting it to her children and grandchildren; who when crises arise meets them unflinchingly and with courage?

Such were these pioneer women. Crude cabins built by their husbands in the 1850s, then when the hop boom came in the 1880s they moved into better homes. But most of these did not have water in them. Water had to be carried from the river or hauled up from wells with a bucket on a rope.

For laundry the clothes were rubbed on a corrugated board using soap made from lye and grease. The lye had to be made first from ashes. A book published in the '80s advised them to soak their clothes in a solution which would save backbreaking work.

The ironing had to be done with heavy black irons heated in front of the fireplace, for all homes had no heat aside from fireplaces. Many had to cook in them, though some cookstoves were available in Steilacoom. The supply was limited as all goods had to come around the "Horn." Mail was months coming the same way and how women did wait for the mail from home to arrive!

The dresses worn were so long that they swept the ground and the petticoats were re-enforced with stout brush braid to prolong the life of the garment. When one watches TV westerns the women are beautiful! How did they keep them clean? The "dress up" dresses were wool or heavy silk and there were no ways of dry cleaning. Young women were taught how to hold up their skirts gracefully when walking, which was not easy. This continued into the 1900s.

These dresses were made with basques which were lined throughout and stays were placed inside around the waist. Corsets were laced up the back and some women tied the laces to the bedpost and thus drew them tight to acquire the wasp-waist so much in fashion in the gay nineties.

All the women had long hair and weekly shampoos were never imagined.

Brushing every night for 15 minutes was supposed to keep the hair clean. Once in six months was the usual schedule for washing the hair. Their hair was beautiful, too. How shocked would one of our pioneer women have been if she had heard of paying several dollars to a beauty operator for a weekly shampoo and set! She would never have believed it of one of her grandchildren.

When candles were displaced by oil lamps, a note in a cookbook assured the women that they were not any more dangerous than candles. But they were urged never to fill a lamp when it was lit. The wicks must be kept trimmed, and explicit directions are given for doing this. The chimneys had to be washed every day as no satisfactory light could come through a smoky chimney. These lamps were to be used for study, for all reading, for sewing, etc. A caution was given not to carry a glass lamp ever, and not to use coal oil to start the fires. Women today like to eat by candlelight but what if that was all the light one had! We glamorize the antique necessities too much.

Shoes were a problem. One article tells of the father making shoes out of pig skins for his children. Mr. Wilton, the little old shoemaker who had a shop where Corbins is now located, used to make stout shoes for children in the 1890s. One girl used to try desperately to hide her shoes under her dresses when she was ashamed of them at school. Women wore high-buttoned shoes and buttonhooks were given with the shoes when they were purchased. Again I read that improvised leggings could be made of newspapers wrapped around the legs and tied firmly. These could be thrown away when one reached one's destination.

Beds were made of ticks filled with wheat or oat straw for mattresses. These had such a clean, sweet smell when fresh and they were much more sanitary than the feather beds brought from the east. Featherbeds were not thrown away to lighten the load for the oxen, on the trek west. Older people, especially, felt that they were a necessity. In 1883 I read that children were better off if their pillows were made of straw instead of feathers.

Pillows filled with hops cured headaches and helped one to sleep. If that failed a dish of fried onions eaten just before going to bed would give one a good night's sleep. Tranquilizers, indeed!

Mrs. Owen's Cook Book 1883 and the *White House Cook Book* 1887 both contain many recommendations for health. As often doctors were too far away women turned to their cookbooks for rememdies.

> Cough syrup: 1 pint of vinegar—break an egg in it, leaving shell and all over night. In the morning it will be eaten except for the white skin. Remove this and add one pound of loaf sugar. Take a teaspoon three times a day. Excellent for any stage of cough.

Diphtheria—sure cure: one-half oz. chlorate potash dissolved in water, add three oz. tincture of iron, one teaspoon in wineglass of water. Gargle with it and after third application the patient will be cured.

If this was effective, what a shame that it could not have been available. Four little graves in the pioneer cemetery, children of Mr. and Mrs. John Kincaid, are a mute sign of the loss of their first three children to diphtheria.

In case of small pox or any contagious disease, cut up an onion, put in sick room, replace every hour. Excellent for disinfectant.

I could write pages eloquent of the makeshift ways women (and men) stood the pioneer life, creating history and laying the foundation for the luxuries we enjoy today.

A few more recipes from the *White House Cook Book* published in 1887 follow: Unvarnished black walnut will look like new if sweet milk is rubbed in with a piece of soft flannel. Sour milk will do.

Toughen lamp chimneys by placing them in a pot filled with cold water to which salt has been added. Boil and then cool slowly—then glass will stand change in temperature.

To prevent lamp wicks from smoking, soak in vinegar and dry thoroughly.

Carpets should be beaten on wrong side first then on the right. Scatter corn meal and salt and sweep to brighten. Straw covered with paper should be laid under them, the carpets stretched and tacked firmly in place.

To take ink out of line, dip spot in melted tallow. Wash out tallow and ink will come with it. Unfailing.

To brighten gilt frames, flour of sulphur added to water till a golden tinge—then boil four or five brused onions or garlic and drain off liquid. Wash frames with soft brush and they will come out as bright as new.

Mutton tallow rubbed on hands at night covered with gloves until morning will keep hands soft and will prevent chapping.

Beat an egg and use for washing the hair.

To clean iron sinks—rub well with a cloth wet with coal oil.

To clean stove pipes—a piece of zinc put on live coals in the stove will clean out the stove pipe.

To banish rats from the premises—use pounded glass mixed with dry corn meal, placed within their reach. Tar is also a good thing to use—put where they run.

Cistern water may be purified by putting charcoal in a bag and hanging it in. the water. No water should be used which has been standing in lead pipes until at least a large wooden bucketful be drawn and thrown away.

CHAPTER 7
QUOTES FROM EARLY LETTERS

These are excerpts from letters written by a homesick 25-year-old wife in what is now the reading room of the library. Little did she think that they would be preserved when she wrote them to her grandmother in Wisconsin. There were only two rooms in the house in 1875 when the first letters were written.

She was the typical woman of the 1870s.

Excerpts from letters written in 1875-78 from Washington Territory by Lucy V. Ryan.

While her husband went to San Francisco with his hops she went to Seattle to stay. They had been married in May 1875 and so far they had no place to live in the valley.

Nov. 5, 1875: I am lonesome, wouldn't take much to make me gray. What fools girls are to want to get married and leave good homes for no home at all. I believe no one in the whole wide world is situated as we are. Have got to make the best of it and just jog along. How I do long for a little place to call home.

Nov. 7: We have just heard some terrible news. A telegraph dispatch telling of the loss of the steamship Pacific, supposed she struck a rock off Cape Flattery, went down immediately with 250 persons all told and a cargo of grain, hops and gold dust. A sailing vessel picked up one man clinging to the pilot house; had been adrift two days and nights and was nearly dead. He was delirious so could give no correct account of the accident.

While a number were lost from Seattle, our principal man in the Puyallup, Mr. Vining, a man highly esteemed by everyone, was lost. He was one of our near neighbors; George thought more of him than any man on the coast. He leaves a wife and eight children. Had all his crop on board. Many of our neighbors had hops on the Pacific and carried no insurance. There were a large number of people from Victoria on board. Oh, it is so sad. The flags on all steamships and vessels are at half mast. I wondered at it a little while ago.

I can't help but feel glad it did not happen on the trip before this one as George went to SF on her. It is the same boat on which we came up in May.

> I will tell you what furniture I have as you want to know. I have a cookstove, one half dozen chairs, and we will make our own table. The dishes are second-hand and mixed, many cracked and handles broken off the tops. There are no knives or forks or cover dishes. I paid $10 in gold for them. Now when I get a broom I shall be made. It is a real pioneer life and how I wish I had some carpet.

After she got into the valley she wrote early in 1876:

> We have men at work so I will have to have a little help as we feed them. I had a China boy but let him go because he was sick.
>
> I own four chickens, two crowers and two hens. Won't we have eggs this winter! I shall sacrifice a crower at Christmas. I must tell you we have a new cow that gives such a lot of splendid rich milk. She is two years old and has her first little new calf, the prettiest little turnip-nosed baby you ever saw. We are teaching it to drink milk. It's so nice to have cream and milk.
>
> A few days ago we lost one of our good horses. Was sick a few hours with colic and died, poor fellow. Wasn't it too bad none of my chickens hatched? Next week I expect two hens off, and some turkeys.
>
> We have four white men and 13 Indians working for us. How they do store away the 'vittles.' I'm glad my stove has a reservoir.

A reservoir is a tank on the back of a cookstove holding water to be heated. This had to be filled every day or oftener.

> We pay hired men $40 a month and board them and poor help they are.
>
> One of the Indian women, Polly, is very sick and they have had 'Tamanis' for three nights in succession. They commence at dark and continue until daybreak. Indian Tom told us this morning that she would have died if they had not had Tamanis. They had an Indian doctor from the reservation. They don't allow any quacks in their practice. If the patient dies the doctor has to run for his life or he will be hanged.
>
> We have several camps right by us. Polly is there. This frightening away the devil is pretty serious for outsiders for they make night perfectly hideous.
>
> I was thinking the other day how little we use our own language outside of our own family. We speak 'pidgin English' to the Chinaman and Chinook to the Indians. This is the trade language, introduced fifty years ago by the Hudson's Bay Company, for use with the different tribes. It is taught at the school in the reservation as well as English.

Indians will speak nothing but Chinook to us. I understand it very well and can talk it enough to get along with them.

July 1, 1876: My ride home from Tacoma with my baby in the bottom of a lumber wagon makes me groan when I think of it. I lay down with the babe on my arm all the way. When I got home I could scarcely move. My girl had supper ready for us.

This mother had gone down to the reservation in a wagon then by canoe to the dock at Tacoma taking the steamer Zepher to Seattle to have her baby. She was called a tenderfoot for doing this.

She continues: "I think when my time comes I shall die and not before."

July 15: We are boarding six men. I pay my girl six dollars a week and don't begrudge it one bit. Today we get mail. It comes but once a week. Address our mail thus: G. H. Ryah, N. W. U. P. & C. P. R. R. to San Francisco, care of P. M. Steamship Co. to Tacoma, W. T.

George is building the first roothouse ever built in this country also the first icehouse. We think by putting water in vats we can freeze a little every year.

July 31: A telegraph line runs through the valley so we can send messages now.

Sept. 8, 1876: We have 16 men to board. There are 250 Indians camped on our farm to pick hops. Some have come 500 miles in full Indian costume and look wild enough to be real savages.

My roses are still in bloom outdoors although Jack Frost has hit them severely. I wish we would sell out here and go east to the Rockys just so I could feel closer to you. Maybe we will.

Sept. 26, 1876: At one time there are parts of 11 tribes, 2000 Indians in the valley, some from the Snake tribe came 700 miles. The Klickitats are great six-footers with thick heavy hair hanging to their waists. They are gay with paint and feathers dressed in the most fantastic manner imaginable. They nearly all carry knives and some tomahawks. There are religious ones, Methodists and Catholic. Sometime I will tell you of going to their meets.

I'm busy as my girl left as she had whooping cough, and I have been trying out lard and tallow and make seven pounds of butter a week. Am using onion syrup for my boy's cough.

Dec. 17, 1876: The excitement of election does not reach us here, we hardly realize the interest and anxiety the election causes. The territory voted for state constitution this fall, so it may be we can vote for the next president.

I sold 10 dozen eggs at 28 cents a dozen in Tacoma. That paid for two dozen two-quart Mason jars with porcelain-lined tops. I'll fill them with plums.

Jan. 31, 1878: A Finn in San Francisco made us a present of a pair of purebred Berkshire pigs from direct importation. They came up all right on the boat from Tacoma.

Chang, our Chinaman, is a kind old man, thinks the world of Harry. When he was a baby Chang would kiss and hug him. How would you like an almond-eyed long-nailed pigtailed heathen kissing your baby? He said when Lewis was born, "Two babies, too muchee, one baby, velley good."

I broke the bows to my glasses and had to send them to SF for repairs. I had them put in steel frames instead of gold so they would not break so easily.

Feb. 8, 1878: Did I ever tell you about our fir bark? It burns like coal, gives intense heat and lasts a long time. The fir trees here grow away up and up. Their tips sometimes touch 200 feet before they send out a limb. Our flag staff is six inches at the foot and two and a half at the top and is 90 feet long.

It might interest you to hear something about Point Gamble where George worked at the mill. This mill is the largest sawmill in the U. S. It employs 200 hands, owns 30 ships and sends lumber all over the world. Their refuse is thrown into a pit which is 100 feet in diameter. The fire has burned in it for 20 years without going out. Several hundreds of cords are carried to it on carts every day. If the poor in the city could only have it what a bonanza it would be for them. 'Tis so easy to make a living here!'

Feb. 12, 1878: The prospect for a railroad across the continent looks brighter. When a railroad is built the eastern part of the territory will rapidly develop. Few people have any conception of the value of the farming land in eastern Washington. Some day Spokane Falls will be the Minneapolis of the Northwest. Here is waterpower unrivaled; it is unequaled in wheat and wool producing; and has the finest forests of fir, cedar, pine and spruce.

Feb. 21, 1878: The birds will tie their stockings around their throats tonight; it's going to be cold. They have warbled since sunrise. One little white-throated songster has sat on the plum tree all day. He will be hoarse when his head under his wing. I love beautiful days and birds just as much as I did when I was a girl with nothing to do.

Shows her character in spite of hardships.

Feb. 26, 1878: Mrs. Kincaid, the lady who lost little Laura with diphtheria, buried another today, Maro, a girl of seven. Her throat filled up and she choked to death. They had five girls and three have died within a year, so sad.

Sept. 14, 1878, Franklin W. T.: We have to keep a heavy watch of men day and night on account of fire. Two hophouses were set on fire and last Wednesday two large barns were burned, one containing 3500 bushels of grain and all of the farm implements. The other had several tons of hay and no insurance. They burned at the same time. We feel so sorry for Mr. Braley, a young married man with a wife sick with comsumption and a baby. He had rented this farm and intended to take his wife to California where her mother lives. Now all he had was destroyed. If the one who did these cruel things is found he will be hung as the men in the valley are quite excited.

Oct. 6, 1878: Did I tell you a man died at a neighbor's during hop-picking? They laid him in a box and carried him to his grave. Not a prayer was offered and the only white person there was this man at whose home he had died. It seemed so sad to me for somewhere he might have had a mother and dear friends.

Oct. 18, 1878: I went upstairs and brought down all my old music out of the bottom of the big drygoods box, the first time I have had it out. It was rainy and I was lonesome and thought I would enjoy fingering the old melodeon again. The next best thing was trying to sing the old songs (so I thought). Up and down went my melodious voice but, alas, I never found a note that I used to know so well. My voice squeaks sadly now. It needs oiling I guess. We can sing 'Home Sweet Home' and 'Greenville' together but that is about all.

CHAPTER 8
EARLY INDUSTRIES

The first store in that part of Franklin territory, which later became Sumner was located in a room adjoining the hophouse of George H. Ryan, now the corner of Main and Ryan Avenue. A picture of his hophouse taken in the 1890s can be seen in the picture file at the public library. The home of the Ryan family, as shown in the picture, is not as it was in the 1870s. Then only the old east wing was built. Ryan and Avery ran this store.

It seems that Mr. Vining had a store by the river about where Meridian Street crosses the Puyallup and that Mr. McMillan had one where he lived southeast of town, but both of them were difficult to reach as there were no bridges.

Some say there was a ferry which could accommodate a team and wagon near where the railroad bridge crosses the Puyallup. Also that there was a ferry at Van Ogles at Alderton, though there was no Alderton at that time. Memories and stories of descendants of pioneers conflict.

We do have a record of a store at this hophouse for the convenience of the settlers between the rivers. Mr. Ryan's daughter, Mrs. Ward Van Vechten, has the old account book of the sales. How the commodities were procured is a question. They must have come from Seattle and there was no road to Seattle. The steamer Zepher brought them to the dock of Old Tacoma. An Indian canoe must have been used to take them to the Indian reservation and from there they could be brought by wagon to the valley.

Supplies were limited but we will look at the names of the customers and what they purchased as put down in the old book, in 1876. Strange prices are given or else the amount is omitted. Every so often cash received is recorded so the bookkeeper must have had to figure the cost of each item when the bill was paid.

In 1876 E. C. Meade was the most regular customer. He bought eggs at 18¢; sugar by the dollar's worth, again and again, no amount given. He also bought pins for how much or how many it does not say; $1 worth of flour; shoes $2.50, socks $1 and vinegar, needles, 44 pounds of bacon @ 20¢ a pound and five yards calico @ 50¢.

B. M. Spinning got coffee, $2.80; one can of lard; shoes, $1.50 and $2.50 along with a pint of syrup. John Kincaid bought two pair of pants at 50¢ and boots for $7.50. The names of J. R. Dickenson, Meeker, L. F. Thompson, Sam Burr, Sherwood Bonney, William Bonney, John Stone and John Boatman appear in 1877.

VanBibber mill is down for something and it is a question in some minds as to where this mill was located. Some think it was at Robert Grainger's place. John Avery, one of the proprietors, bought a pair of boots for $6. A queer note of a "new deal" with Sherwood Bonney April 23, 1877, seems to have something to do with labor. Beans, bacon and merchandise to Mr. Purvis is recorded in 1889. W. P. Wood's name appears then too. J. H. Wright bought brown sugar.

This store may have been run only during hop-picking and that other times settlers had to ford rivers or cross them on ferries to get to a place where food could be purchased.

There is no record of a store in this vicinity before 1876. The story has been handed down that two Jews ran this store for a while, but this cannot be corroborated.

An interesting item appears in the old account book of the payment to Jonathan McCarty of $250 for acreage to be used for an experimental farm. This dream did not materialize. The *Herald* tells of the purchase of this land north of the Stuck River, but as no farm of this nature ever occupied this land, who owned it after McCarty sold it? We do know that the Harris family lived on this farm in the early 1890s. More about this family in a later chapter.

John Avery acted as justice of the peace and the only record of an arrest was of John Stone for driving his mule faster than a walk across the new bridge over the Stuck.

Some day we will take a walk along Main Street after places of business and homes are erected, trying to get a picture of life as Sumner grows into a village.

SUMNER INDUSTRIES IN THE 1890s

Jan. 3, 1890, *Sumner Herald* quotes:
  Enterprises that furnish employment to hundreds of men.
  Brief sketches of that which is and that which is to be.
  Phenomenally rapid development of one of the best sections of the west.
  Manufacturing and fruit growing, a basis of wealth and prosperity.

We have given a brief description of Sumner, her favorable location, the quality of her soil, of her religious, educational, moral and healthful influences. This is not all that Sumner possesses to commend her to those in quest of good locations in which to establish homes, and perpetuate the race. Besides having all the qualifications formerly ascribed to her, Sumner is one of the greatest manufacturing places of her size in Washington.

MANUFACTURING

Principal among the many manufacturing industries of Sumner is that of the Sumner Lumber Company, an enterprise owned and operated by Messrs. Geo. H. Ryan, E. T. Everett and W. J. Madden. The company owns about 5000 acres of land mostly on the hill east of Sumner, heavily timbered with fir and cedar from which to supply their mill with logs. They manufacture all kinds of dressed and rough lumber, hop boxes, fruit crates, shingles, waterpipe, etc. The company enjoys an immense patronage which is rapidly growing larger. Their mill is rushed to fill all orders. The Sumner Lumber Company has the confidence of all its patrons.

It was established in 1883 and incorporated in 1885. The capacity of the sawmill is 25,000 feet daily with planning capacity 15,000 feet.

The mill camp of workers consists of the following and their families: J. C. Wright (Dock), T. A. Wright (Anderson), Dave Wright, Phylander Wright, Sam Farmer, Abe Dean, Charles Cones, Sam Lott, Jim McCloskey, Bill Fix, Frank Beerman, Henry Woodside, Thomas, Erickson, McKay, Dibble, Porter, VanClive, and others. These men were employed as edger, N-bearer, carriage, skid-greaser, burner-stoker, carpenter and driver of teams. Henry Woodside handled the main saw and lost his arm in consequence.

In the 1890s the sawdust and slabs were burned instead of being used for fuel. A fire was kept burning night and day at Salmon Creek and a dump cart filled with sawdust was drawn by Slacker, an old reliable horse, to the fire.

The slab wood was put on a truck which was pushed by hand down the inclined skid road to the fire. Today we would consider this a great waste. Pictures of this mill are in the scrapbook in our library.

A plank road about two miles long was built by the Sumner Lumber Company to Sumner. The planks were 16 feet long, 12 inches wide and four inches thick. It was called by the editor of the *Herald* "The Boulevard de Plank" and will be featured in another chapter. When the mill burned in the early 1890s some of the cabins were moved into town. Dock Wright bought one for $1.50.

This mill, giving employment to many was one of the things that started Sumner on its way to becoming an important town.

SUMNER MANUFACTURING COMPANY

One of the heaviest stockholders and the manager of this establishment is Mr. F. W. More, a gentleman who bears the enviable reputation of being the finest workman in wood known in this country. This company manufactures doors, stair casings, mouldings, and all kinds of inside finishing material besides plain and fancy ornamental work with both inside and outside finishing.

The fact that the Sumner Manufacturing Company is furnishing material for several brick blocks now in process of construction in the city of Seattle speaks volumes in praise of the company's work and reputation. This company furnishes employment to from 15 to 30 skilled workmen all year.

The building in which the business is conducted is 70 x 110 feet but the present size being inadequate to the rapidly increasing patronage, a second story will soon be added to the entire building, making it the best-equipped and most extensive establishment of the kind in the state.

THE SUMNER EXCELSIOR WORKS

An industry that is designed to be one of the first and best paying in Sumner. The entire plant is just now having been recently put in by Messrs. A. Grossman and C. E. Stewart, two enterprising young men from New York. The factory is well equipped for business. All of the machinery is of the latest and most approved order. They have over one thousand cords of the finest article of sun-dried cottonwood on hand for manufacturing into excelsior. When well under way the factory will furnish employment for several men. The demand for excelsior is good and the industry cannot do other than prove a lucrative one.

SPRINGVIEW BRICK AND TILE FACTORY

The latest new enterprise established near Sumner is that of George Atkinson and Mr. Raymond, formerly of Puyallup and is called the Springview Brick and Tile Factory.

Mr. Atkinson is an "old timer" on the brick clay question. A few months ago he made the valuable discovery that on land then owned by Geo. H. Ryan was to be found the finest quality of fire brick clay known to exist west of the Rocky Mountains. He at once negotiated and purchased the land.

Mr. Ryan is considered a shrewd business man but Mr. Atkinson rather "did him one" when he purchased from him the finest brick clay land in the country. However, the joke is on Ryan, and he is not to blame for not knowing the fine qualities of the land. Ryan has dealt in lumber not in brick.

Atkinson and Raymond are hustlers. They have already cleared their land, prepared fuel for firing, and will as soon as spring opens, begin with a large force of skilled workmen, the work of moulding 20,000 bricks daily. They will burn several kilns daily during the summer. They have put their clay to several tests and the results are such as to enable them to authentically state it is fully as good, if not better than that from which the world renowned Philadelphia pressed bricks are manufactured.

Verily the "Springview Brick and Tile Factory" has a "soft snap."

Sumner has several other minor manufacturing industries that should be mentioned in connection with the foregoing, but space forbids such mention in this issue. There is, however, one other great industry of which we will make a brief mention.

VEGETABLE AND FRUIT GROWING

Sumner is of all points in the great state of Washington the home of all fruits and vegetables. Without taking the space in which to name the many varieties of fruits and vegetables, we will cover the ground by asserting that they are all produced here to a greater degree of perfection than anywhere in the known world. The market for those products are first class. If doubting persons desire further information, we refer them to Messrs. E. C. Meade, H. M. Williams, W. V. Mcfarland, and A. W. Stewart, all of this place. We could mention dozens if necessary.

In the fruit and vegetable seasons·scores of hands are employed in preparing the products for shipments. And after all expenses are paid the growers' net profits amount from four hundred to seven hundred dollars per acre for the land cultivated.

In view of these many and never-failing industries, we hesitate not in saying to all persons who desire to establish good homes in a good and life giving climate and country, COME TO SUMNER, the God-favored portion of the great state that bears the immortal name of the father of his country.

An early settler said that the people of Sumner should be very thankful that when flood comes the high water does not affect Sumner as it does her sister cities between Seattle and Tacoma. "While the people of Auburn and Kent are going to and from their meals in boats, the water in our town is not within 25 feet of flooding. It is the highest point in the valley, being 30 feet higher than Puyallup." The above was written for the *Herald*.

In 1875 few of the donation claims were fenced. The fact that they were of irregular shape made it difficult to tell where one piece of land touched another. The roads meandered along wherever it was easy to travel. There was quite a controversy over the roads.

In fact, it never was established legally from Stuck Bridge to Elhi. It followed the line of least resistance. It bisected the 40 acres which George H. Ryan had bought, following the ravine through to Abraham Woolery's. (This is now Wood Avenue).

The road ran straight from the ravine to the Presbyterian church (the corner of Traffic and Main now). This was opposite the John F. Kincaid home. Dr. George F. Whitworth surveyed what was to be the town and said the street should be 40 feet wide. John said, "I am not making any allowance for the standard road. We will let the road widen as it is needed, the land is not worth anything anyway." Mr. Ryan bought seven acres from John Kincaid north of what is now Main. At that time it joined his 40.

As Mr. Ryan owned the bisecting road across his place he wanted it fenced. Sam Burr agreed to give 15 feet for a road and then Mr. Kincaid finally gave 15 feet so the road could go down Main Street from Meeker to the Presbyterian church, now Main Street.

For three years the men worked on this road grading and raising the height until it was even, so the ravine could be fenced. When the fence was built a stile was placed at the corner. I remember it well. It was a set of steps to pass from one side of a fence to the other without opening the gate. How many people in Sumner ever saw a stile? I wonder! Mrs. Artemisia Andrews, our poetess for so many years, wrote a poem about the orchard path. I quote the first and last stanzas of it:

"The Orchard Path"
Tis only now a memory—that winding orchard way
Where lovers lingered in the shade of apple boughs asway
When the pale moon cast silhouettes of leaves upon the grass,
Like joys that quiver o'er our hearts, and with the morning pass.

Ah, how we loved to dally on along the mossy tract,
Wishing it were a journey far with ne'er a turning back.
And fancying the fruit, that swung so gaily from the trees
Alladin's jewels or the apples of Hesperides.
Where once the path trailed idly, now there lies a straightened street,
The little lads have grown to men and walk with sobered feet.
The lovers gather now around their home fires' ruddy glow
In cozy cottaages, fair set in prim and painted row.

No street more fair is any—where, no homes more good to see,
But how I long to tread again the path that used to be—
The little vagrant heedles path like wandering winds astray;
But now 'tis just a memory, that winding orchard way.

This was published in the *News-Index* Jan. 14, 1921, and she wrote that the old winding path was being graded for paving that week.

Listening to Murray Morgan tell every morning of the urban renewal projects in our neighboring city brings to mind that the 1890s property owners simply went out and brought their properties up to standard without any supervision from city officials.

Sept. 26, 1890 a very amusing item appears, quote:

Passengers will no longer have to climb over or under freight cars to board the train as the NP has built a platform for the milk cans—it will be no sin to worship it as there is nothing like it under the sun; Ryan calls it the Democratic platform. We advise our readers to only risk one eye at a time when gazing on it.

One can read between the lines that people resented the way the NP treated Sumner.

Dec. 5: Wednesday, a party of enterprising citizens residing on the street which runs from Main to opposite Lenover's livery stable to the campus of Whitworth College turned out and graded that thoroughfare in fine style. The procession was headed by Torn Lenover who furnished a team and did the plowing. Half a dozen others followed with shovels and mattocks taking out stumps and roots, leveling the street. We commend these citizens and hope others will follow their example.

L. F. Thompson is removing his large hophouse to near the site of the proposed new hotel where it will be used as a livery and fee stable."

A decent street crossing from the bank to the opposite side of Main street has been leveled. Another is badly needed from the Sumner Pharmacy to Hillman's market.

Dec. 12: The street leading from Main past the Christian church and on to L. F. Thompson addition was plowed this week by C. M. Darr and will be graded and leveled in a few days. Now let us get sidewalks on all streets.

Jan. 2, 1891: In compliance with a suggestion made by the *Herald* a few weeks ago, a sidewalk has been constructed between the Sumner Pharmacy and Hillman's Market. Pedestrians can now glide along dry show where they used to wade in mud to the knees and in some places higher.

F. Swenson has material on the grounds for the construction of an eight-foot sidewalk along the street fronting his property. His example should be followed by every property holder in town. W. R. Lindsay is building a fine sidewalk along his elegant residence.

This residence is the apartment house now next to Nicholson's Pharmacy. It was moved from Main street years ago.

Jan. 30, 1891: A board with SUMNER in large letters was placed on the depot this week.

Feb. 6: The incandescent lights of Puyallup were lighted for the first time four days ago. Sumner should follow their example.

March 13, 1891: E. Meeker of Puyallup is thinking of extending his electric light wires to Sumner. If we can't think of a better way he had better do it!

March 27: At the council meeting a point near the McCarty farm in Stuck river was designated as a garbage dump.
    The council voted to let people close alleys and streets for gardens but consent must be in writing.

April 17, 1891: We are glad the water tank and depot have just been given a new coat of paint as President Harrison will soon be passing through here.

June 5: Dr. C. W. Stewart came before the council asking that in grading Cherry street the cherry trees be not damaged.
    "Woodman, spare that tree,
    Touch not a single bough;
    In youth it sheltered me,
    And I'll protect it now."

The editor quoted this from McGuffy's reader. The council voted to spare the trees.

Sept. 7, 1894: The crying need of this town is a sidewalk from Ryan's hall to the depot. One end is in ruin and the other a mudhole. Something should be done before someone is killed or maimed for life.

Fences were being built as cows roamed the streets. G. H. Ryan installed a street lamp in front of his bank block. Other oil lamps were placed because an order was given to the marshal to light them every dark night. We wish we knew how these lamps were financed.
    Grant Shipley and his brother Levi were lamp lighters and had the task of trimming, filling them with oil, cleaning the chimneys for the six that were placed on Main Street. They would seem like dim lights today but many a fall was averted and many a pair of shoes kept clean because of their rays dispelling the darkness.
    A picket fence surrounded the Ryan home on Main Street. This fence had been built in 1877. A row of butternut seeds was planted along the street but only one grew. This was the famous historic tree the city removed last spring

(1963). It was planted by a homesick bride who longed for her Barraboo, Wisconscin home with its trees which she loved.

Another beautiful old tree stood at the corner of Thompson and Sumner Avenue. This too was taken out years ago. Joyce Kilmer wrote truly, "Poems can be made by fools like me, But only God can make a tree."

CALAMITY STRIKES THE BUSINESS DISTRICT

Main Street in the 1890s was quite different from the Main Street of today. There may have been just as much activity, though of a different sort. Wagons drawn slowly along, sometimes runaways, teams tied to the hitching racks in front of the livery stable or the blacksmith shop after the horses were given a drink from the watering troughs.

Main Street was so muddy that the *Herald* says, Feb. 27, 1891:

> The planking of about three blocks of the business section of Main Street would prove a great convenience.
> In June 1890:

G. H. Ryan has for some time past had in contemplation the erection of a fine two-story brick building on his property east of Rewey's hardware store on Main Street. Monday we were shown plans by Charles Lowe, the architect and contractor. We predict it will be one of the handsomest structures in the valley.

Twill be 50 x 60 feet with front elevation 35 feet. There will be three store rooms on the first floor 18.6 x 50, 20 x 50 and 20 x 50. A bank room 19 x 50 will occupy the SE corner. There will be a stairway in the center six feet wide leading to a hallway six feet wide on the second floor running the length of the building.

In the NW corner of the second floor will be the Masonic Lodge room 32 x 36. In the SW three offices 11.6 x 19.6, 19.6 x 10.6 and 12 x 9.6. An office in the center will be 19 x 10 and one in east end 14 x 15. The front will be glass and brick with galvanized cornice. Work has begun and home concerns will furnish all except glass and hardware.

This building will mark a new era in Sumner as all buildings before this have been constructed of lumber. Now what we need is a first class hotel open to the traveling public. A stock company should be organized to get us a hotel.

Work began July 25, 1890. The brick was furnished by Springview Brick and Tile Co., the lumber by the Sumner Lumber Company, mill work by F. W.

More Manufacturing Company. This brick was the first made by the new firm in their kiln.

By the first of 1891 the offices were filled by the following: Sumner Lumber, Light and Water Co.; the bank which had been incorporated the first of the year by W. L. and F. E. Thompson and E. C. Meade with a capital of $25,000, Will Thompson, president, E. C. Meade, vice president, W. H. Paulhamus, cashier, and Fred Thompson, secretary. The vault was large and fireproof with a burglar-proof safe with a time clock, all of which gave the community confidence in the new bank, and made it worthy of patronage. (They paid $30 a month rent).

The post office under T. B. Darr paid $25; the barber, W. R. Messick, paid $25; Bergman, for his store, $25; Dr. Stafford. $10; Driskell $10; dentist Williams $5; while the city council had free use of a room. It is interesting to note in an old bookkeeping book which ones were marked "paid!"

However, in 1895, Aug. 30, an account is given in the *Herald* of the terrible fire which swept the north side of Main Street and wiped out all of the buildings.

> At 9:30 p.m. fire started in the upper story of the old hardware store and when the alarm sounded (which was the ringing of the church and school bells) in a few minutes over a hundred men had gathered and had begun to fight the flames with water in buckets. The brigade could not reach the upper story but they fought valiantly until the fire department No. 1 from Tacoma, which was sent out on a flat freight car arrived. They pumped water from the NPRR watertank. The old hardware store was dynamited trying to save the other buildings but when it fell it burst into flames and only added to the conflagration. In the meantime the occupants of the stores on the south side of the street were being evacuated, everyone helping to carry out furniture and equipments. Two times the drugstore caught fire as did also the other stores but the flames were extinguished saving the buildings.
>
> The whole inside of the brick block was ablaze when the wall fell in. If this had not happened the whole town might have gone up in flames, at least the east side. The contents of all buildings were saved though damaged.
>
> What was the origin of the fire? No one knows. Some thought that a cigaret had fallen down under the wooden sidewalk where some young men had been singing an hour before. But that was ruled out when it was remembered that the fire started in the upper story. The most plausible theory was that a spark from the engine which had passed through at 7:15 had ignited and smouldered until the roof was ablaze. It hardly seemed possible that a tramp had crept up there to sleep and had acci-

dentally started the fire. Many think it was the work of an incendiary. However it might have been worse.

Sympathy goes out to T. J. Lenover and E. T. Everett as they were heavy losers and were not insured. Also the butcher shop, livery stable, and barber shop did not carry insurance.

The hardware store and billiard room, owned by Maria Remington of Tacoma, were insured for $150, about one third of their value. The Ryan block was insured for $2500, about one-half of its value. Everett's stock, valued at $500, was a complete loss not insured. Henry Church's stock insured for the $2,000 was paid $800 insurance. The Sumner bank was fully insured for the $100 they lost.

Across the street, Maloney's building was damaged $200 but was insured. W. W. Wilson and R. A. Guffy were fully insured for the loss to their buildings. Mr. Guffy's furniture was all carried out and returned after the fire. Thomas Farrell saved all his tonsorial fixtures. Mr. Arnot lost a few tons of hay from his livery stable.

The Tacoma fire department stayed until all flames were extinguished, which was not until morning. B. F. Day, the mayor, had a note of appreciation and thanks to them in the next week's *Herald*. The W. W. Wilson family also inserted a "thank you" to those who carried out all their household goods and returned them after the fire.

A. E. Wright rebuilt his blacksmith shop at once and was ready for business. Henry Church moved a hophouse to the corner and had it made into a store building which was used for many years. Several hophouses were brought to Main Street and fitted for occupancy so stores could function as soon as possible. Main Street had a poor appearance for many years because of the fire.

F. S. Dobler, resident agent for the German-American Insurance Co., was pleased that his company paid claims so quickly. It spoke well for the company.

Nov 15. 1895, a night watchman was hired to patrol the streets to keep watch so another conflagration would not appear. H. S. Church advertised goods damaged by the fire at special prices.

New telephone poles were soon laid on the ground ready to replace the ones burned down the night of the fire.

The burning of Main Street caused many a heartache not recorded and brought problems that took many years to solve. But the true pioneer spirit the Sumner business district rise again to serve the community, though she never has had the business that she would have had, had she not been planted between two large cities easy of access.

CHAPTER 9
RYAN'S HALL OR THE OLD OPERA HOUSE

In 1882 Henry Church and Will Thompson, energetic young men, conceived of the idea of having a skating rink built in Sumner. They promised to pay George H. Ryan $1,000 for such a rink and $25.00 monthly.

Mr. Ryan agreed and bought lots from the Presbyterian Church on Main Street adjoining the R.R. track. He built this rink next to the church. It was 80 x 40 feet. Charles Lowe was the contractor. The floor was of W. G. fir, 1 1/2 in. thick laid from the center out so the tread was on the grain. It was planed and sandpapered by hand.

The truss holding up the roof was unique and when the building was razed in 1963 it still held east to west but still leaned from south to north so the boards were spreading apart making it a hazard to passers-by. Handmade square nails were used throughout.

The opening night 100 skaters were on the floor, many coming from Tacoma and other towns. The young men thought they had a bonanza and paid $100 the first night, but the bubble burst and never another cent was paid. Mr. Ryan turned the rink into a public hall with a stage. It was available to any organization or person. For the worthy cause he often gave its use gratuitiously.

In April, 1891, the death of Hansford Wright, a 17-year old boy stirred the whole community. There was no church large enough to hold all who would wish to attend the services. Mr. Ryan offered the use of the hall. Reverend Maynard conducted the services before a crowded house. School was closed and teachers and pupils attended in a body. The sawmill closed for the funeral because several of the boy's brothers worked there. Many beautiful floral tributes were presented and interment was in Sumner cemetary.

Many forms of entertainment were held in Ryan's Hall. There were no electric lights as Sumner was still without electricity. Lamps hung from the ceiling and around the walls giving a dim light for all kinds of affairs from political meetings to church services.

Magic lantern shows were common in the 1890s. When the public school gave Evangeline in 1898, Virgil Goss and I read the poem while the pictures were shown.

Whitworth College held its annual commencement programs in the hall. Socials of all kinds were given by the different churches. Ice cream socials were the most common and the Methodist women gave one almost every week.

Perhaps some reader might not know how the ice cream was made.

Women came in the afternoon bringing cream, eggs, whole milk, sugar, flavoring and cakes. Ice was bought from the butchershop in gunny sacks. The freezers were packed with alternate layers of mashed ice and rock salt around the can in the center.

When filled, the dasher and the cream mixture were placed in the can and the top put on: the handle was turned round and round until the dasher could no longer be moved. Occasionally the ice had to be pounded down with a broom handle and more ice added, while the water ran off through a hole in the side of the freezer.

Youngsters would sit and turn the handle for hours for the privilege of "licking" the dasher. Several freezers would be turning at once. This ice cream was sold for 10 cents a dish and served with a generous slice of cake.

Ice cream today cannot hold a candle to that homemade ice cream when a young swain treated his best girl. A former member of the Methodist Church, Mrs. Lou Doherty, says that the first Methodist Church was paid for by the turning of the ice cream freezer.

Who can remember the old-fashioned box social? Women and girls brought a box supper and each was auctioned off to the highest bidder. Often a man who wanted to buy his best girl's box was made to pay a pretty sum as rival bidders egged him on.

There were concerts, literary programs, lectures, all kinds of entertainments, not forgetting political rallies.

Dec. 19, 1890, the Presbyterian and Methodist Sunday schools united in a Christmas tree. Parents were invited to bring their children's presents to the hall and they were promised that these would be hung and distributed by Santa Claus. Each child would wonder if a beautiful doll or sled or wagon was to be hers or his. The presents were not wrapped and made quite a showing, but many a child went home disappointed when his name was not called.

That same week a temperence meeting was held for all churches. Dr. George F. Whitworth preached and over 100 signed a pledge not to drink wine, beer or cider. Another union temperance meeting was held the next Sunday when the Reverends Davenport and Davis preached.

A rather humorous item in the *Herald* said that skating rinks like bustles belonged to a former era.

A christmas program and cantata were given when Edna Kincaid portrayed winter, E. D. Swezey, Santa Claus, Henry Wellington, time. The trio's singing was highly appreciated. About 40 children, gathered around a simulated fireplace, sang carols, hung stockings, then retired. Santa came and stuffed the stockings and went back up the chimney. The children returned and happily received presents and candy. This was also given to every child in the crowded house.

As an example of the way the editor described an entertainment I shall quote just one which is typical.

> The entertainment given Wednesday night under the auspicies of the Presbyterian Ladies' Aid in Ryan's hall was a successful affair, socially, artistically and financially.
>
> The hall was neatly decorated with plants and honeysuckles. At 8 p.m. the programme opened with a solo, entitled 'Spring is Only Love,' by Mrs. A. E. Cook. The rendition was characteristically excellent and was loudly applauded. Mrs. Cook has a singularly sweet, rich and flexible voice.
>
> Prof. E. D. Swezey's baritone solo, 'Comrades', was given with precision. Prof's voice also possesses much flexibility and purity of tone but it was scarcely under as good control as he usually holds it.
>
> Mrs. C. C. Johns' solo was rendered with sweetness and delicacy having fair range but slightly indistinctness of enunciation."
>
> "Oh, Solomon Levi," by the quartette Fred Purvis, A. G. Wellington, Prof. Swezey and C. C. Johns was immense and elicted much laughter and applause.

The editor thought of himself as a music critic!

> The chief attraction of the evening, to be sure, was Col. Will Fife. The fame he has acquired in his appearance as a tragedian in our neighboring cities created a desire on the part of the people of Sumner to hear him. (A prophet is not without honor save in his own country, etc.) Their expectations were in no way disappointed. The rendering of 'On the Tennessee' was touching; for his perserverance to fulfill and the audience was held spellbound. Also the 'Death of Benedict Arnold' was exquisitely rendered. The entire entertainment was highly appreciated and enjoyed. Col. Fife deserves the thanks not only of the entire community for his perserverance to fulfill his engagement and for his gratuitous services to the good cause of the Ladies' Aid.

Often the receipts were as high as sixteen dollars.

In my story of "The Old Opera House" April 18, 1963, in the News-Index, I went into detail describing the Whitworth College commencement programs. I also told of the Decoration Day celebrations and various other forms of amusement, which took place in the hall. It was truly the center of all social life in the comrnunity in the "horse and buggy" days.

The Don Zechs bought the property from Sumner Steele in 1929. For 35 years they have served Sumner with their garage and gas station. The building had to be torn down for safety's sake. Now a modern gas station has risen to take its place to serve the community in a far different manner from the old hall.

Eighty-one years is a long time for a building to be in constant use. Like people, buildings when gone are finally forgotten by succeeding generations. However, memories of good times in the old hall still "linger on" in the minds of a few old timers.

CHAPTER 10
PEOPLE OF THE TOWN

JOE THE CHINAMAN

During the 1890s a great many Chinese were imported to work in the hop fields and for the railroad. They worked for less pay and lived very cheaply. White men began to think that if the Chinese were not here there would be better times for them. A wave of hatred arose climaxing in the expulsion of these innocent foreigners.

There were about 2500 of them in Pierce County, many living at Alderton and in Puyallup. A few worked in Sumner helping women with their housework. Some amusing stories have been told about the Chinese cooks. One lady asked her cook how he got such a nice brown on his pies and to her horror he took a mouthful of water and spewed it over the pie before putting it in the oven. She decided not to ask any more questions, but told him not to do that any more.

When men decided to drive out the Chinese, posses frightened them by setting off dynamite by their houses. One Chinaman named Joe worked for Frank Young, who lived across from the old cemetery. His daughter Emma and Angeline Parker cut Joe's queue and hid him in the brush on the hill. Mr. Young threatened to shoot the men who came for Joe so they left him, the only Chinese in the valley.

When the Youngs moved to Yakima they took Joe with them, but he did not like it there and returned to Sumner where he lived on Elizabeth Street until his death in 1916.

Jim Wigton, who lived at the west end of Elizabeth Street, was a friend of Joe's and when Joe wanted a wife he sent for a matrimonial paper and Joe began a correspondence with a lonely woman. Joe had to get some boy to write his letters for him and a picture was sent of Mr. Young's son making the woman believe it was a picture of Joe. She consented to come west and marry him and he sent her money for clothes and her fare. When she arrived Joe was waiting, wearing a red flower in his lapel as he had promised so she could identify him. She took one look and fled to Mrs. Ludlow's hotel when she saw he was Chinese.

Some women took her under their care and she finally went east and was married. Joe continued to work his truck garden, was an honest, hard-working man. Boys played jokes on him but he was good natured and minded his own business, paid his debts and was well thought of by all. He married a woman with several children and was good to them.

One woman remembers how a beautiful doll was admired and wished for by all the little girls as it was displayed in a window and how surprised and envious they were when Joe bought it for his little girl.

MISS JANE COLE

A never to be forgotten lady familiar to many in Sumner as she drove her pony cart about peddling her butter and eggs was Miss Jane Cole.

Born in England, she was a seamstress for the royal family in London before coming to America with her brother Edward. She loved to tell of making dresses for the princesses. I had a room in her home and often listened to her stories of taking a sick child up into the hills for it to regain its health.

When they came to Sumner from Michigan, they rented the Abraham Woolery farm. Miss Cole had been working in the linen room of the old Tacoma Hotel in Tacoma. On the farm she took over managing the hens and cows while Edward ran the hop field.

Mrs. L. F. Thompson was her first customer when Miss Cole began to sell eggs and butter. Laura, Mrs. Thompson's daughter, had married Will Fife and lived in Tacoma. She promised to get customers from the best families there if Miss Jane would deliver her products in Tacoma. So she became the "butter and eggs" woman driving Billie, her pony, the nine miles every Saturday. As it took the whole day, the little girl who always accompanied her grew very tired.

The child was the daughter of Ralph and Mable Lenover and when Mable died, Miss Cole became like a mother to little Faye, who lived with her until she was married. Mary Munro had come with the Coles from Michigan and she also lived with Miss Cole until her marriage to Miller Cooper.

Later the Coles lived on the Bonney farm until Edward's death when Miss Jane built the house which still stands on Academy next to the Presbyterian church. Later she built the one on the corner and one on Alder where she died.

If we go into the 1900s we will remember how much Dr. and Mrs. Mitchell thought of our dear lady. She cared so tenderly for a sick boy of the Mitchell's.

The doctor was with her the night she passed away. She had been a "doorkeeper in the house of the Lord" for years, acting as custodian for the Presbyterian church. Mrs. Swezey and I were with her that last night and she kept saying, "Peace, wonderful peace." When she breathed her last, I ran over to the church, as service was going on that evening. It did not seem strange that as I entered the door the congregation was saying, "Peace, Wonderful Peace, the Gift of God's Love." Could anything be more appropriate as a lasting tribute to a woman whose life had been a real testimony to her faith in God?

DR. SPINNING, THE PIONEER DOCTOR

A familiar figure on Sumner's streets during the last years of his life was little old Doctor Spinning. He had served as physican to three Indian tribes, his territory extending from Vancouver, Washington, to Vancouver, B.C., from the time he was appointed by Gov. Isaac Stevens in 1862 until his retirement. He then bought property at Dieringer and built his home overlooking the valley. He was happy to be near his old friends and relatives.

He was called an herb doctor, using roots, plants, etc., which he procured in the soils. His grandchildren remember helping him gather cascara bark, Oregon grape roots, etc. There were no drug stores and his method for curing the sick was popular with the Indians and many white settlers. He had graduated from the Eclectic School of Medicine in Cincinnati.

Smilingly, he drove his horse down the plank road, waving his horse whip at the group of children who always shouted a greeting, as he was well liked by them.

Later he built a home where the city hall is now located. He and his wife Mildred were charter members of the first Christian church organized in the territory. They remained members there as long as they lived. Mrs. Spinning was a wonderful woman. She used to assist him when he brought a new baby into the world. One admirer of Mrs. Spinning tells how when she was immersed in the Christian church, Mrs. Spinning, helping her dress, reminded her that she had dressed her when she was born. Both the doctor and his wife were dearly loved and as long as he lived Indians, even though they had free treatment at the hospital, continued to come to him for advice.

When Dr. Spinning was dying he sent for young Dr. Karshner who was just beginning his practice in Puyallup and laying his hands on Dr. Karshner's head, he said, "I hereby bestow on you all my powers of healing." This was the manner of Indian witch-doctors and Dr. Spinning's close contact with them influenced his action.

CHAPTER 11
EARLY SCHOOLS

The first school house was built on the Abram Woolery DLC in the 1860s. It was built of logs and the cracks were filled with mud. Crude shakes were placed on the outside and a fireplace was made of clay and sticks. The benches were logs split in half and smoothed with a broadax; four sticks for legs were placed in holes bored with an auger in opposite sides. If backs were desired, the benches were placed against the wall. There were no desks so slates and books had to be held on the laps of the pupils. The house was about 12 by 16 feet.

The first teacher was Miss Laura Kincaid, the youngest daughter of William M. Kincaid. The next teacher was John Meeker, Ezra Meeker's brother. One night when he was the teacher the schoolhouse burned from a spark in the chimney, so John took the children to his own home where he taught them for the remainder of the term. His house stood where Oz Rogers now lives.

The pupils were Jacob F., Daniel H., and William H. Woolery, William D., Sarah B., and Nancy Owen, James F., and Joseph C. Kincaid and Frank Carson who rode from across the Puyallup River on horseback.

The next schoolhouse was built on the NE corner of Wood and Main streets (there were no such streets then, it was in the midst of a forest). It had real windows and a door. It was made of rough sawed boards and battened. It was about 20 x 23 feet and was used for all public functions, debates and community Christmas tree programs.

A letter from Mrs. E. Palmer Spinning (Mrs. Ben) told of her coming to teach in this school in 1877, in district 8 as it was called.

In 1877 a two-room schoolhouse was built south of where the Sunset garage now stands. John Hall was the first teacher. His pupils were Lydia Woolery, Johnny Woolery, Lettie Boatman, Horace Baker, Luella Kincaid, Fred N. Bonney, Emma Young, Etta and Lucy Baker.

Jonathan and Ruth McCarty had taken their children to Seattle where there were good schools. Their daughter Clara had graduated from the University of Washington in 1876, the first and only graduate. She taught school and became the first woman county superintendent of Pierce County. She visited all the schools even going to the peninsula in a boat she chartered. She deserves to be mentioned in our story of Sumner as she was a Sumner girl. A new hall in the university is named for her.

Quote from the *Herald* March 28, 1890:

Never in the history of Sumner public school has that institution flourished and prospered better than during the present term which began the first Monday October last.

The teachers were Prin. Orville Moore, intermed. Miss Mary Wellington, and primary Mrs. Moore. The enrollment had been larger than ever before, and the daily attendance excellent.

Monday morning of this week, Prof. Moore tendered his resignation to take effect Friday. This was something of a surprise to the trustees who think Prof. Moore should finish his term which will close in June. Clerk R. A. Giffy says there was a verbal understanding that the teachers were hired for nine months. Prof. Moore says he was employed by the month and as school boards are usually not slow to ask a teacher to resign when he proves unsatisfactory it appears that a teacher should exercise the same rights. Prof. Moore goes to Snohomish at a much larger salary. Mrs. Moore also resigned as primary teacher and unless teachers can be secured at once to fill the vacant positions our free school will be left in a deplorable position.

In the *Herald* of May 9, 1890, L. F. Thompson suggests that a new school building to cost not less than $10,000 be completed by the first of 1891. He favored an extra assessment for this and that it be extended over a period of 10 years.

May 16, 1890, a note says, "A new schoolhouse is a real necessity." The town was growing and after the prosperity from the hop boom, sentiment rapidly spread that it was high time to build a good schoolhouse.

June 27, 1890: The children of the public school had a gala day under their teachers Miss Nichols, Miss Wellington and Prof. Tait. Through the courtesy of Mr. Ryan Esq. the entertainment was held in the Opera House. Parents and all interested were invited. Tables groaned under the load of good things. After a program of exercises, recitations and essays the children feasted to their hearts content, their only regret was that they could not get outside of more good food. The Rev. Davenport asked the blessing before dinner. Mr. Coy, Mr. Shipley, Mr. and Mrs. Williams, Mr. Ruel Sr. enjoyed themselves as well as the youngsters. Prof. Tait gave the scraps to an Indian family gladdening their hearts also.

On July 4, 1890, there was quite an article about Lake Tapps wanting to absorb part of the Sumner district taking in Milltown.

July 5, 1890, an election was held to vote bonds for the new school building. Eighty-one votes were cast, 78 for and 3 against. "It is good to know that it was almost unanimous."

December 19, 1890: Material for the foundation for the new school building is being hauled giving work for several Sumner teamsters. The weather being favorable the brick work is progressing rapidly. Let us have the corner stone laid with an imposing ceremony. Sumner doesn't have many chances to put on 'other clothes' except on Sunday. We have several local orators who could do justice to the occasion. What say all of you?

Aug. 22, 1890: The schoolboard hired Leonard Tait as principal, Miss Anna Funk from Spirit Lake, Iowa, as intermediate teacher, and for the primary Miss Mary Wellington. The principal was to receive $100 a month and the ladies each $60. Miss Funk comes highly recommended as a teacher and a lady—the others had been previously employed (so no compliments).

Sumner Herald Feb. 13, 1891:

A magnificent temple of education is under process of construction— the finest mechanism ever seen on a public building in Pierce County.
    Designed plans and specifications as made by G. C. Clements & Co. of Tacoma accepted and adopted by our schoolboard are accurate and complete in every detail. Contractor Driskell is following them to the letter. When completed it will be the finest and best appointed school building in either Pierce or King County, aside perhaps one each in the cities of Tacoma and Seattle.
    The Emerson school building in Tacoma was the inspiration for Sumner's new edifice.
    Bonds of $40,000 were voted to replace the 'shack' now in use. Seen from passing trains it will be the best advertisement Sumner has ever had. Every acre in the valley is increased in value 15 to 25% by the erection of our fine new school which shows confidence in the present and faith in the future of our fertile vale.

Feb. 27, 1891: G. C. Clements has disappeared. Where? No one knows. But in spite of the absence of the architect and contractor, the work on the new building goes beautifully on.

March 13, 1891: The new schoolhouse is ready for roofing and weatherboarding. Miss Nellie Purvis was hired to teach in 'overflow' in the old reading room as the school is so crowded. The board is very wise in selecting Miss Purvis as she is a very successful teacher. A flagpole 36 feet high will rise on the steeple of the new building.

May 15, 1891, a board meeting was held in the new schoolhouse.
As I attended high school in the new building in 1892 my recollections of the old schoolhouse will be personal.

I had finished grade school in Slaughter so was ready for high school when we moved into the VanTassel house on part of the Hayward DLC at the foot of the hill where the slaughter house now stands.

There were no buses to carry children to school, so we thought nothing of walking several miles. My sister, brother and I, with our lunch in a 10-pound pail, were joined at the first corner by Helen and Kenneth McFarland. When they grew old enough my sister and the twins Bessie and Jessie Johnson were with us, too. Austin Parker (Pike) came out from his home also on the Hayward DLC. The Parker home was south of the plank road.

At the Ames home (now the Lantz place) we were joined by Bessie and Perly whose parents had come from Boston in 1892. Their older sister Clara later married W. Q. Brown, principal of the high school.

Now my little brother was becoming tired so he would take our lunch bucket and run on ahead and sit down on it and wait for us. I never could see how he gained anything, but his fat little legs seemed to gain strength by the few moments of rest. He did that several times on the way.

The Sydney Williams children were not old enough so we passed on to the Kirkwood home (now the Perfield place) where Allen, Agnes, Aleck and Matthew were usually added to our crowd. Marian, Ralph, Robert, and Frances were not yet old enough. Marian is the only one of this family still living. They had come from Scotland in 1891. As we rounded the corner the Horner children, Ross, Myrtle, Charles, Roy and Blanche, came running with Holly crying to come too. At the next street crossing Alice Clarke met my sister Margaret as they were fast friends for many years.

When we neared the railroad crossing, Bessie, Helen and I used to walk the track trying to stay on the rails without stepping off. Then if we kept on five rails we held our breath, to see what boys we would meet—not that we felt it might decide our fate, it was just fun. Simple amusements satisfied us in those days.

I remember with what keen enjoyment we girls sat under Prof. Dewey's teaching of English literature. His big black eyes shone as he helped us understand poetry. The memorizing of parts of "Thanatopsis" and other poems was real joy for us to recite to him. Pearl Darr, Bertha Powers, Helen Johns, Emma Young, Jennis Clarke and Clara Engdahl were the girls I think of most as absorbing poetry.

Henry B. Dewey was an uncle of Gov. Thomas E. Dewey of New York. When the school board let him go after he had signed a contract, he sued the district and won. He asked for the full $1,000 but the court gave him only $550. However, he gave it back to the district as he only wanted to show he was unjustly fired. He went to Tacoma where he had a better position and become county superintendent.

When I taught in Sumner in 1898 to 1901, he came often to visit our rooms and was very kind and helpful. He was a fine man and Sumner was fortunate to have had him when the school was getting a real beginning that first year in the new building.

It was truly a fine schoolhouse. The wide halls and wide stairways made it possible to empty it in a few minutes for the weekly fire drills. Windows on two sides of every room gave splendid light and the colored transoms ventilation. Fifty seats allowed ample room for the two grades which occupied every room.

At the ringing of the bell, the pupils of each room lined up in two lines at assigned entrances. Every one of the four doorways was entered by an orderly marching group keeping step to the beating of the triangle and the piano in the lower hall. There was no scrambling to rush in. Mr. Tuel, the janitor, rang the bell for five minutes at 9 and at 1 o'clock. Some children were not allowed to leave home until the bell began to ring, thus they were kept out of mischief.

In the three years I had as fellow teachers, Maime McFarland, Alma Bacon, Adah Hunt, Lenora Manchester, Olive Hubbard, Virgil Goss with W. Q. Brown and Mr. Protzman as principals. Often we took our lunch up to the belfry where we could watch the playgrounds and enjoy the view, and each other's company.

I wonder if any of my old pupils recall the time each one deposited a little green frog on my desk as he entered? The frogs did not stay on the desk, they hopped under the steam radiators, down the aisles, under the desks where they were crushed or cooked. Mr. Brown, entering with a quizzical smile, answered when I asked if he had seen these frogs when they were in line, that he had, but that he was told I had asked for them. I had asked for polliwogs so we could watch them turn to frogs! I'll leave it to your imagination the way we solved this problem.

The teaching profession was quite different then. We took an examination at the courthouse in Tacoma, and passing received a certificate and taught without any practical training. Thirty dollars was the salary and that was usually discounted when we took our warrants to the beautiful old stone courthouse and climbed to the top floor to get our money.

A copy of the report of Sumner schools by H. B. Dewey at the close of the 1892 school year is very enlightening. Added to the names I have already given are Mary E. Crawford, Mrs. M. R. Thayer, Anna Funk, Mrs. Agnes Cook, Marion Corkery. The directors were chairman George H. Ryan, J. C. Kincaid, E. C. Meade and T. B. Darr, clerk.

State Superintendent Bryan during his inspection of the new building said:

> It is as well arranged building as I ever saw. The arrangement of the light is perfect and I consider it the best school building in the state for the number of scholars it is designed to accommodate. The property has cost a great deal of money but it is worth all it cost and years hence it will stand as it does today an ornament to the town and source of satisfaction to the people.
>
> The financial condition of the district is not a very satisfactory one. The balance sheet shows a deficit of $48,000. Why? Because the county commissioners levied a tax of three mills instead of four as heretofore. Because the levy was made on a supposed valuation. This was afterwards cut down. Because country contiguous to Tacoma was annexed to that city and the school taxes were paid to that district and not to the general fund of the county. We began the year with a deficit and have made extensive improvements which are permanent. This depleted our treasury. Other villages in the county are similarly situated.
>
> We still own the old school site, its value is nearly as much as our deficit. We deem it advisable to hold it until we get a good price. The number of pupils enrolled was 260.

This property was where the Sunset Garage is now located and the land south of it.

This old building, loved by all who attended school there took fire in the upper story in 1924, whether from sparks from chimney or combustion will never be known. The fire department and citizens fought valiantly to save it, to no avail. The first units of the Wade Calavan school had been built so school could go on.

The cutting down of some of the old maple trees which surrounded the school yard was lamented by those who had considered them part of the beauty of Sumner.

In 1907 an amusing item appeared which stated that slates had been abolished and parents felt that pencils and paper would be a great expense.

Band concerts from the cupola of the schoolhouse were enjoyed by all the citizens of Sumner for many years.

CHAPTER 12
EARLY CHURCHES

White and Rousseau, editors of the *Herald*, in 1890, wrote: "Truthfully it has been said, 'Schools and churches are the mile-posts of civilization.'" Sumner is plentifully supplied with both, of the latter she has three."

Christians went first to Steilacoom to worship and when schoolhouses were built they were used as gathering places for services. The Prebyterian church edifice in Sumner was dedicated in 1878 and the Christian Church having been organized in 1853 on the prairie between Longview and Gravelly Lake was organized in Sumner at nearly the same time.

Most of the charter members of the Steilacoom church had moved to the valley. They were Israel Wright, Thomas Wright, Abrial Morrison, J. R. Meeker, and Sherwood Bonney. Members had been baptized in Gravelly Lake; Mr. and Mrs. B. F. Wright were the first converts. Mr. and Mrs. George H. Ryan were baptized and united with the Christian Church in Sumner in 1879.

Previous to 1877 the Presbyterian Church was a branch of the Presbyterian Church at Steilacoom as the record written by Dr. George F. Whitworth in the minute book shows.

The Presbyterian Church stood on west Main and the Christian Church was built on the corner of Alder and Maple in 1883, having 80 members at that time. Just a few years ago a new Christian Church was erected near the Maple Lawn school on the outskirts of town.

The directory given in the Herald in 1890 records that the pastors in Sumner were: the Rev. D. M. Davenport, Presbyterian, the Rev. Henry Cogswell, Christian, the Rev. T. J. Massey, Methodist, the later services being held in Ryan's hall.

The Baptist Church met irregularly until 1904 when it was organized and baptismal services were held in the Stuck River until the church was built in 1905 and dedicated in June 1906, according to an item in the Herald.

The following were the pastors of the Presbyterian Church until 1900: Previous to 1876, the Rev. George W. Sloan; 1876, George F. Whitworth with seven members; 1882, F. C. Armstrong, 15 members; 1884, George A. McKinley, began Oct. 1, 1883, 92 members; 1887, Rufus Patch acted as minister and moderator; 1887, Aug. 6, J. G. Watson; 1888, D. M. Davenport, salary $1,000; 1898, E. R. Pritchard.

In accordance with instructions of the Presbytery, a committee of the session was appointed to confer with the session of the Puyallup Church in regard to having a pastoral union with that church. The moderator, Dr. Calvin W. Stewart, president of Whitworth College, with elders Fish and Swezey were chosen to act on this committee.

It was decided to ask the Reverend Pritchard to divide his services equally with the two churches. He rode his bicycle between Sumner and Puyallup until 1899 when the Rev. Robert Boyd began to act as stated supply and then as pastor. The Reverend Pritchard continued as pastor at Puyallup. He was called the "sweet singer of Israel" as he had a fine tenor voice and added much to the music of the community. He was pastor until the early 1900s.

The lodge directory given in the same Herald follows: A F & A M Sumner Lodge WD, meets each third Monday of the month at 8 p.m., G. L. Gray, WM.

The IOOF meets every Saturday evening E. T. Young N.G. March 13, 1891, quote: "Work is progressing on the new Methodist Church."

This was built on the northwest corner of Wood and Washington Streets and is now the Free Methodist Church.

April 1, 1891: An ice cream social will be held in Ryan's hall by the Methodist ladies tonight.

The house in which the John Porter family lived at the sawmill camp was purchased by the Methodist Church for a parsonage, Frank Young moving it to the church property.

A social given by the Methodist ladies at the L. L. Benbow home was a magnificent success. Dr. Corliss rendered guitar solos with excellence.
A luxurious luncheon was served.

This was in 1895 and one could fill columns with stories of the socials held to earn money to pay for the new church.

Sept. 7, 1894, records the Reverend Gray who had had charge of the Methodist Church for two years was leaving to enter Evanston University in Chicago. He and his wife had endeared themselves to the people of his charge and he had won the confidence of the entire community. He was a young man of fine natural ability and "we expect him to take a leading place in his denomination."

Sept. 14 the Rev. George W. Landon was appointed to take his place. Watch night services on New Year's eve were always held, all churches uniting. A revival campaign was held every year by the M. E. Church.

It was a great day for the Methodists when the mortgage burning took place September 1, 1899. Women had worked strenuously raising money enough to bring about this event. Rev. Gray and others were honored by memorial windows placed in the new church.

These stained glass windows were brought to the present Methodist Church and are enjoyed by all who attend services there. The actual burning of the mortgage was done by Mrs. Priscilla Dobler and Mrs. Anna Cagley under direction of the pastor, Rev. George Arney, who had led in the effort to raise this mortgage. The Sumner Herald gave an account of this event in 1899.

In 1922 the old church was sold to a Japanese group who held services in it until the second world war and the Japanese were placed in a concentration camp in Puyallup. The misses Nora Bowman and Ethel Hempstead, former missionaries to Japan, had been working with the group in this church. The building was then sold to the Free Methodist congregation and their remodeling and changes have made it almost unrecognizable to those who loved it in the early 1890s.

An early settler said that Sumner was founded on the church and truly it was the center of all life from its beginning until modern amusements and other organizations rivaled its influence.

This history will not try to record events later than 1900 therefore the churches who came into being later will have to wait for another historian to tell of them.

In the little crossroads church—

CHAPTER 13
ENTERTAINMENT

People devised ways to enjoy recreation in the 1890s as there were no parks, no bowling alleys, no swimming pools. As the only means of transportation was with the horse or the bicycle, most of the good times centered around the home.

All the boys in Sumner vicinity had great sport in "the old swimming hole" as it was affectionately called. More's Pond was on the More donation land claim. When Robert More filed his claim he built his home on the bank of the Puyallup River. When the river cut into the bank, it undermined the house and formed the pond right where the house had stood.

The story of the cutting of the pond is Mrs. Edith More Herr's and I shall quote her:

> A log jam formed in the river about where the city dump is now and a big spruce tree was forced into the bank tip first. The surge of the flood kept forcing the trunk of the tree up and down, back and forth, ramming it into the bank; the water did the rest. That tree remained there until the dredging of the river for flood control. As the river cut a channel to the north it was jiggled by each high water till it moved against the east bank where the swimmers used it as a diving board.

I have been told the boys wore no bathing suits and girls were never known to go swimming.

Stone's Landing, or as it is now named Redondo, was the Mecca for camping and almost everyone in the valley went there each year to spend a week or two. The water was cold but the most courageous one ventured in for a dip in its icy depths. To rent a boat and row across to Maury Island to see the lighthouse was often part of the fun.

Evenings a huge bonfire was built on the beach where the campers, leaning against the logs, accompanied by the sound of the waves, sang and talked until late hours. Beds were made of fir boughs laid on the ground and were not too comfortable, but that was part of the fun.

Improvised stoves for cooking would astonish campers of today with their barbecues and sleeping bags. There were no people living at Stone's Landing and it was very unusual to find any other group camping. Pictures of some of these parties may be seen in the library. In the files of the Sumner Herald, news items tell of Sumner folks camping at Stone's.

One year the local Union of Christian Endeavor spent an entire week holding meetings, sunrise services on the beach around a bonfire and vespers there. Young people from Orilla, Kent, Slaughter, Buckley, Puyallup and Sumner were in this union which was led by Rev. O. L. Fowler. All pastors took part in this convention and it left a lasting impression on the ones who were there.

All-day picnics were popular at Stone's Landing, too. The Stewart wagon had seats around the wagonbed and with buckets of cherries, eating these and laughing, much of the day would pass without getting out of the wagon except for lunch.

The 4th of July in 1898 we had reached the top of the hill above the landing when a passerby told us news had come that the Spanish-American War was ended.

Arthur McKinley made Addison Stewart, who drove the team, stop and before we could go down the hill we had to memorize every stanza of "America." I can still remember every stanza and have been thankful for that patriotic young man who was responsible for that experience.

One year six of us had to walk all the way home the entire 15 miles through the woods as the wagon went on ahead when we walked up the hill to save the horses. That walk would make an interesting story in itself. We sang "Juanita" all the way, for we said we would sing it until we caught up with the wagon, which we never did.

Those who took that walk were Rollo and Belle Everett (they had been married only six weeks), Ernest Darr, Harry Ryan, May Stewart and Amy Johns (myself). Mrs. Stewart was very upset over this when we reached their home because she felt it was too long a walk for us.

The green of the hills and the valley was beautiful before advanced civilization brought changes and we enjoyed the loveliness of our surroundings. When the Milwaukee Railroad came through and the hill was cut away, it was almost a heartbreak for those who had enjoyed its beauty as it sloped down to the valley. Now there are those who feel the same way about the freeways changing our valley, but one cannot stand in the way of progress.

HORSE AND BUGGY DAYS

I am glad I was born in the "horse and buggy" days. The perspective of the past has always influenced my present. These memories of the 1890s will be personal, even quotations from the Herald bring back memories of scenes never to be forgotten by those who lived them.

I was used to horses from my childhood in Iowa because we had a horse something like Dapple of 20 years ago in Sumner. Dapple, the beloved horse of children who learned to ride on that broad back, will always hold a warm place in the hearts of children who used to slide down her tail. This Welsh pony belonged to Connie Rogers! But Sumner had a horse well known in the 1890s too. His picture is shown in the story of the sawmill camp by Lennie Ferguson published in the *True West* magazine last April.

Slacker was his name, so called because when worked double he let the other fellow do most of the pulling. But Slacker was one horse who went to college. He was smart enough to open any gate so he roamed the streets and the grass on the college campus looked good to him. He would wait until classes were called and then open the gate and have a good time grazing. One day the boys caught him and tied tin cans to his tail. He beat his record that day by running 25 miles per hour. He never went to school again.

Slacker was the first mail carrier in Sumner carrying the mail between Sumner and Puyallup. W. P. Wood rode him and one day Slacker slipped on the river bank and went down into the Stuck, and the mail was never recovered. The Ryan boys were want to tease the hired girl by leading Slacker into the kitchen (now the children's reading room in the library).

When we moved to the VanTassel place at the foot of the east hill in 1892 we had a fine, gentle horse named Prince. I used to hitch him up (the only difficulty I had was getting the crupper under his tail!) to drive to town.

There was a hollow sound accompanying the trotting of a horse on the plank road and we could always tell when our father was coming by Prince's hooves beating time until he came to Parker road when the sound stopped. A corduroy road (made of slender saplings laid on stringers side by side and not nailed down) went from the corner of our barn. A swamp had to be crossed, for there was no drainage system then.

When my boy friends came to take me to parties at Parkhursts on the hill (now Mountain View) or up the west side of the valley, over a narrow, dark, muddy road to Stewarts', they would leave their horses hitched to the fence at the corner and walk in for me. It required skill to manipulate a horse over a corduroy road.

Horses had to wear mud shoes when plowing and often a horse would mire down in the pasture and a team would have to be used to extricate him.

We had another pony, a yellow mustang whose name was Tat. He was unpredictable. One day when my mother and I were driving to Sumner a horse in the Parker pasture began to race with us. Tat took the bit in his teeth and away he went like the wind. My mother could not hold him and called out for me to help. So I took the reins ahead of her hands. By the time we reached the Kirkwoods, Tat calmed down and we rode sedately into town. Once I put the sidesaddle on him and with my long skirt hanging down rode into Sumner. Then Tat took a notion to trot all along Main Street and on to the depot with me bouncing up and down, a spectacle which caused me much embarrasement. I never rode him again.

Black Beauty and *Beautiful Joe* were popular books at that time and we were aware of the mistreatment of horses. Often I surreptitiously slipped the cheek rein loose when I found a horse tied, with his head up in the air. Many a time I remonstrated with a man who was beating a horse who was trying to pull too heavy a load. We tried to get blinders taken off bridles, too.

The *Herald* records in 1891 many run-away accidents. I shall quote a few of them to give modern day folks an idea of scenes common in the early nineties.

> D. M. McKinnon's team ran away in the reservation, scattering vegetables for miles, the profits of months of hard work. The team finally ran into the ditch and one horse suffered a broken neck. Our sympathy is extended to Mr. McKinnon.

> T. B. Darr's team driven by Mrs. Darr accompanied by Mrs. Cook and Mrs. Wilson was frightened by one of the women raising a parasol and attempted to run away, but was stopped by a quick jerk of the lines which drew the horse and wagon against the fence by the roadside.

> W. P. Wood bought a heavy team of horses 1400 pounds each. They had been shipped to Puyallup direct from the Oregon range. He left with his threshing crew for Kent. Later this powerful team ran away, frightened by a freight train, spilling several gallon cans of milk on the way to the creamery.

> E. C. Meade's team ran away upsetting the dearborn and wrecking the wheels, breaking the harness, and demolishing some raspberries. Mr. Meade had trusted them to stand without tying while he talked to Sam Cagley about crates. The trusted team became fractious and with heads up and tails over the dashboard moved down the street so fast they could not be seen for the dust they raised.

> Mrs. Will Spinning was driving along Main street and had great difficulty holding her dapple dun in check as he, seeing old faithful cutting capers, became exceedingly agile; but the lady holding the reins was mistress of the situation. Mr. Meade's horses were stopped at Smith's Blacksmith shop on west Main and the wagon and harness went into repairs.

John Kincaid's horse ran away on Pacific Ave., Tacoma, when the buckling of the holdback strap let the buggy run upon the horse. When the buggy struck the curbstone, Mr. Kincaid fell out and suffered scalp wounds and had a cut knee. Willie jumped and was kicked by the horse. Dr. Corliss makes a dash with his dandy little span of ponies. Our sporty doctor is the swiftest Jehu "what they is" when seated behind his spirited little team.

Jan. 30, 1891: W. B. Carville and Frank VanFliet, carpenters, were moving to Orting. They hired a large black horse from W. V. McFarland and a brown pony from A. H. Woolery and a wagon from C. M. Darr. They forded the Puyallup just above the Querry ranch. After unloading and letting the horses rest and be fed Mr. Carville started on the homeward trip. Upon reaching the river he found it had risen, but apprehended no danger. Half way acorss, the wagon box and Carville were lifted from the running gears of the wagon and started down the river.

Carville, falling into the water was nearly drowned but managed to get into the wagon box. The team going down the river both horses were drowned. The Querrys heard Carville's shouts and rescued him with a boat. Our sympathy is with the young men. The McFarland horse was valued at $150 and the Woolery pony $40 and the wagon about the same."

Mr. Harris's horse ran away on the Stuck bridge and the wagon was demolished, but no one was hurt.

April 10, 1891: W. H. Paulhamus returned to his paying-teller job at the bank, bringing with him his wife, a fine driving horse and his household goods. They will live in a cottage owned by Henry Church.

In the same issue: Ye editor is a good horseman but when it comes to riding a wideback horse miles over a rough and rugged road he is not a success. He did this Monday of this week and hasn't been able to get his feet within a yard of each other since, besides having something like spinal meningitis.

A. M. Rousseau was the editor.

There were many reports of men riding up into the mountains prospecting. About 600 men were working around Eatonville. Many long stories were written about trips to Echo Lake on horseback as almost every man owned a horse.

In the early days Will Fife was talking to Mrs. Lucy Ryan and she was very discouraged. Said she, "We will all end in the poorhouse."

"No, Mrs. Ryan," said Will, "You will be riding in a carriage and I will be living in a brownstone mansion some day."

She did own a carriage in the 1890s but it was almost a village-owned carriage for she loaned it to every funeral and even weddings. In her diary she records many times: "Died today. I must go and see if they would like my carriage for the funeral." Will Fife did not live in a brownstone mansion but could have, no doubt, if he had so desired.

The *Herald* of June 20, 1902, records:

As the Ryan carriage was returning to Sumner from the Ryan-Johns wedding June 18 one of the whiffletrees fell down on the horses' heels when crossing the railroad on Main Street. This scared them so badly that they ran away, upsetting the carriage and the occupants were violently thrown out. Mr. J. W. Wood was picked up unconscious and the other occupants were severely bruised and shaken up. It is fortunate that no one was seriously hurt. Mrs. Ryan had just remarked, "I am glad we have reached home safely!"

By 1898 it was feared that bicycles would supercede the horse. An editorial expressed the reasons why this could not be:

Bicycles cannot travel over bad roads; they are not beautiful nor interesting; are unhandy to use at night except on well lighted streets. They are liable to puncture, often at great distance from home. The wheel can carry but one rider and it requires great exertion to make it go and often gets off balance. It's bad for trousers and skirts; the riders must have special costumes for riding. The idea is perverse and absurd that it will supercede the horse. On the other hand it benefits the horse by having better roads made, will keep the horse out of unfit hands; will reserve the horse for those who love and appreciate him.

Now the editor gets poetical when he thinks of the bloomers which became popular with girl bicycle riders:

Will the bloomers all bloom in the fall tra la?
   When wheels are in fashion again?
   Will the 'new girl' go back to the skirts of her ma
   Or put on the trousers of men?

Our editor speaks his mind again on fashions:

A good comment on the size of the modern dress sleeve follows: A young man rushed to the aid of a female cycle rider who had taken a header but unceremoniously took to the woods when he discovered in his excitement he had attempted to help her up by her bloomer sleeve instead of her dress sleeve!

The bicycle craze has hit the boulevard de plank. Aerial exhibitions are often seen as riders are cavorting and careening. Everything is free even the ditch.

In May, 1897 a bicycle parade took place on this boulevard and photos were taken. "Miss Lydia Manchester and T. B. Darr took a spin to Roy and back (some ride!). H. S. Church bought a new Butler bicycle."

This was interesting to me as our first ride in a horseless carriage was in Henry Church's Franklin. We sat in a little high seat in the back in 1902.

Will Darr bought a new Falcon last week.

A meeting was held and a petition to the county commissioners for a bicycle path from Sumner to Puyallup was passed. The Sumner Bicycle Club elected the following officers: President, Henry Church; vice president, R. E. McFarland; secretary, H. R. Ryan; treasurer, T. B. Darr. The dues are 25 cents a quarter in advance, funds to be expended on the bicycle path. B. S. Fryar offered to grade one mile at their end. That will leave but one mile for the club to grade. Members were urged to donate one or more day's labor. Let every one 'ginger up' and help carry this project to a finish.

The path was constructed of cinders. The little Presbyterian Minister E. R. Pritchard was to be seen on his bicycle, whiskers blowing in the wind, as he rode back and forth between his two charges, Sumner and Puyallup. Once in a while a tandem could be seen but it never became popular as a girl taken for a ride by her boy friend felt that she could not control the direction they traveled and she did not enjoy being in such a subjection to the stronger sex.

An item quoted from the *Sumner Index*, June 1, 1902, shows us that bicycle riders found riding over the sidewalks was not easy:

If the city marshal continues to build new and repair the old sidewalks in the manner as those already built and repaired it will be but a short time until the pleasure and convenience of a wheel will be a thing of the past. Whenever a new sidewalk has been built it is either higher or lower than the one adjoining making a jumpoff or a jumpup, which is unpleasant for the rider and injurious to the wheel. These walks are being built in patches and until all can get their walks rebuilt we do not see why a little respect should not be paid to the wheel-riders by dispensing with these jumpoffs.

CHAPTER 14
DECORATION DAY

The observance of Decoration Day in the 1890s was quite different from its observance today. I shall try to give you a picture of the day as I remember it. I shall quote from the *Sumner Herald* which gives us a glimpse of what this day meant to the entire community.

> May 29, 1890: young girls went from house to house with clothes baskets gathering flowers, which were taken to Ryan's hall. Young women there made them into bouquets. At 9 o'clock May 30 almost everyone in the town formed a line to march to the cemetery. Usually it was a hot, dusty trip and the flowers held in warm hands were wilted by the time the march ended at the cemetery. Patriotism in the hearts of the marchers still soared high as they marched behind the old soldiers led by the bugle corps.
>
> The Civil War Veterans wore natty uniforms showing signs of age, but the slouch hats decorated with a laurel wreath of real gold, sat proudly on each hoary head. As they walked they remembered the hard tack (a hard dry cracker) which had been their principle food during the war. That could still be purchased in the grocery stores in 1890 and we used to munch it remembering Civil War days. These old soldiers received a pension of $12 a month until 1890 when it was increased to $20.
>
> All girls were asked to wear white dresses when the whole school marched under the guidance and control of the teachers, Miss Nichols, Miss Wellington and Mr. Tait in 1890.
>
> Flags had been placed on all the old soldiers' graves early in the morning and each received one of the bouquets, after appropriate ceremonies were conducted.
>
> The Puyallup GAR post met the Sumner post at the gate and participated in the ceremonies.
>
> At 1:30 the public school board, clerk and all teachers met to be photographed and had to exercise much patience waiting for the sun to come out from behind a cloud. In a body they then marched to the hall where a mound of moss was covered with flowers by each child depositing one in memory of a departed soldier.

A program of speeches, vocal numbers and instrumental music was listened to with great pleasure by the elders, but many a child grew restless as the speaker of the day eloquently orated on the debt owed to the soldiers who had fought so earnestly for their country. A text from the Bible which was often used was Isaiah 43: 6: "I will say unto the North, give up, and to the South keep not back." Added to this was the phrase "Give up anger and keep not from friendship."

In 1890 Swezey and Stewart and Misses Kirkman and Wellington with Mrs. Will Thompson composed a quintet which sang several numbers. Miss Viola Kirkman magnificently rendered "How a Horse Won a Battle." The Hon. T. Hueston gave an edifying lecture. A band concert followed, after which a family picnic was held by the river or at Boatman's grove or Grainger's.

GAR Programme of Everett post No. 73, 1892, quoting the *Herald*.
Here we will interject an historical fact not very well known. GAR was the first alphabetical abbreviation used in the U. S. Today we are used to hearing ADA, UN, NATO, etc.

Elaborate programs were printed for Decoration Day in 1892. The observance was held Sunday, May 29, and Monday May 30. The memorial service was held in the hall, with the following program: Grant, 95th Psalm; Cho., "Work for the Night is Coming"; prayer and reading of scripture; quartet, "They Rest in Peace"; sermon by the Rev. Mr. E. R. Hayward, text, Matt. 26:7.

Monday May 30: Cho., "Strew the Garlands"; prayer by the Rev. D. M. Davenport; D. M. Davenport; exercises by GAR post; solo and chorus, "Battle Hymn of the Republic"; address C. L. Fogg; music, "The Iron Cross," college orchestra; recitation Mrs. Will Thompson; quartet, "The Red, White and Blue"; benediction.

Officers of the day, President G. H. Ryan, vice presidents W. L. Thompson, E. C. Meade, J. C. Kincaid, B. M. Spinning, Alex Gow; secretary H. B. Dewey; marshal, L. R. Coombs.

Committees: arrangements, Misses Funk and Crawford, Dr. E. A. Stafford, F. McFarland; programme, Reverend Hayward, Profs. Dewey and McNair; speaker, Messers. Guffy and Ryan; Sunday servies, Messrs McFarland, Horner and Guffy; Music, Messrs. E. T. Everett and Charles Baker; hall decorations, Miss Luella Kincaid, Carrie Wellington, Charles Baker, Charles McFarland, Rollo Everett, Henry Wellington, and E. D. Swezey.

The members of the post were F. McFarland, R. A. Guffy, John Tuel, I. T. Darr, George T. Meyers, Charles Mullen, W. W. Wolff, C. Cotton,

W. A. Horner, H. A. Marble, A. D. Cline, Henry G. Lott, J. B. Kraus, E. R. Hayward, W. H. Kingery, D. W. Dobler, C. M. Darr.

It is interesting to note that these men were from companies in the following states: Illinois, Iowa and Wisconsin, Kraus and Kingery were in the cavalry.

This faded old program can be seen in the history file at the library where each man's company is shown. The deceased members of Everett post 73 are given also and the officers of the post. Commander was F. McFarland; Adjutant R. A. Guffy; vice commander, G. T. Meyers; officer of guard, John Tull; junior vice commander, G. T. Meyers.

The 1894 Memorial Day celebration was described in the *Herald* as follows:

Twenty grizzled veterans, heads frosted with age and ranks perceptively thinned, aroused sympathy of survivors and keep reverence for those who had given their lives in defense of the Union. Hymns were sung by Agnes Cook, Belle Johns, M. C. Powers and Ernest Darr. They were sublime and beautiful. This program was given Sabbath evening by the GAR and WRC.

Wednesday the Woman's Relief Corps gave a sumptuous repast in the Shipley building. Coral and Blanche Marble sang a duet, May Darr gave a recitation, Mrs. Cook and M. C. Powers sang a duet, Myrtle Tuel gave a recitation and Bessie Ames rendered a violin solo. The meeting was closed by all singing "America."

Entertainments meant much when there were no amusements as we have them today. Sumner was one happy family, sharing each other's joys and sorrows. With all our inventions for making work more simple, we today do not have as much leisure time as did those early citizens. Are we better off than they?

CHAPTER 15
PIONEER CEMETERY

As I slowly walked in the sacred old pioneer cemetery, just east of the mausoleum, scanning names on the tombstones, stories of early experiences as told to me by descendents of those buried there swept through my mind.

Stories are told of how it came to be the burial place 100 years ago when this valley was still a primeval forest and of the heartbreak of parents who found pioneer life too hard for little ones. A few homes (cabins) had been built and when death came to some of the children, the question arose, "Where shall they be laid to rest?" At first four little children were buried at what is now North Puyallup. At that time it was called "The Devil's Playground" because the Indians had a resort there where they met to gamble. Some whites used to take part also in this sport. A description of the way they gambled would make a story in itself.

In time it was thought best to have the road pass right over where the four children were buried. The great hearts of Isaac Woolery and his wife Mary prompted them to offer two acres of their donation land claim for a burial place.

Each family had to move its own, so three families dug up the little caskets and carried them to the new cemetery. One family refused to do this so the pavement at North Puyallup passes over what remains of the little body of the fourth child.

Dewey Coffman and I searched for the three graves, Dewey brushing away the moss from the little stone markers. We read George W. Whitesell, age 3, and Alex H. on the same stone, 1861-1864 and 1877- 1878. A little lamb was molded on top of the marker, its meaning clear: "He (Jesus) carried the lambs in His bosom."

The same little lamb was found on a stone for Alice Woolery, age 4, and E. M. Sherman, age 3. As we walked on we found so many little children's graves.

"Twin boys and Vivian, darlings of F. A. Carson," also the son of E. S. Stone which showed us the area was large from which people came to bury their dead in this cemetery; these two families were from what is now Puyallup and Alderton.

Four little markers bearing the inscriptions 8 mos., 4 yrs., 2 yrs., John, and 2 mos. were the children of John and Nancy Kincaid. Diptheria took these four, all in a year's time. My mother-in-law, Mrs. Lucy V. Ryan, wrote to her grandmother of this tragedy and how her heart ached for the Kincaids. John Kincaid was the grandfather of the Swezeys and the son of William Kincaid.

As Dewey brushed away the moss on the old tombstones we found many names of the men who incorporated the Pioneer Cemetery, April 23, 1877. The articles of incorporation were signed by George B. Kandle, auditor, Washington Territory.

These are the men who formed the Puyallup Valley Cemetery Association:

A. H. Woolery 1825-1899. Listen to what we read on his stone: A. H. Woolery and his wife Mary (Aunt Pop, as she was affectionately called) "Altho' he sleeps, his memory lives, But cheery comfort to his mourners gives, He followed virtue as his truest guide, Lived as a Christian, and as a Christian died."

Olive's name is also inscribed on this marker. Another Woolery stone had carved hands clasped on top—M. A. Woolery and F. Woolery mutely speaking of love for each other.

W. W. Sherman, age 72 years and John F. Kincaid 1838-1897.

R. S. More—and there again we felt the heartbreak of the death of two children, Alice Myrtle, age 7, and Charles More, age 20, in 1889.

W. J. Bowman (from what is now Puyallup), D. M. Ross (his claim was where the experimental station is now located), John Carson the first postmaster of Franklin (the name of the valley post office). There we read "Willie May, age 9 mos. and 7 das."

Other signers were Gawn Grainger, C. W. Stewart, A. J. Miller, J. R. Dickenson, Lynus Burr, L. F. Thompson and W. B. Kelley. (Many Kelley names appeared, among them Mary Kelley.)

E. C. Meade and Laura, his wife. Their names recalled that when he lost his wife and his home he went to Alaska. The record reads "Burried in Alaska." Many old timers felt that he died of a broken heart. ("Burried" is the way it is spelled.)

C. C. Henners, and we looked in vain for the marker for Willis Boatman but on inquiry discovered that his body was placed in the mausoleum and that his wife's was also moved there. However John, Millie, George, Lucy and Effie Williams, also Lettie Williams, lies beside her husband, Henry Williams. John was the child stolen by Indians when 3 years old and found unharmed later.

Z. A. Stone—we found a marker for son of J. J. and E. S. Stone. (Stone's Landing was named for the sons of Z. A. Stone.)

J. P. Stewart—his claim was across the Puyallup River from John Carson's. He was a school teacher and later a merchant in Puyallup.

W. C. Kincaid and John Carson. We found names of many other early settlers in this old cemetary. Florence Evison 1879-1896; one wooden marker had rotted off at the base, 1886-89, but the name was illegible. The Bonneys,

William M. Kincaid, 1799-1870, and his stone had carved draperies over it, his daughter Ruth and her husband, Jonathan McCarty, and F. C. Seaman. His stone had a Mason insignia inscribed on it. It was his 40 that G. H. Ryan bought after his death. Mrs. Laura Seaman was married to E. C. Meade later.

For Thomas LeMarr, age 25, we find "His sun went down While it was day, Yet to the upright There remaindeth light in darkness."

Nathanial Searles and family, Rufus Patch, James E. Bell and wife Debbie, Reuben Baker and his wife Sarah and their marker had "gates ajar" carved thereon as did several others, a mute testimony of entrance to Heaven. Robert Low, 70, died in 1891; Margaret Ally, age 20; Alex Gow, 1895.

We could have registered many other and well-known settlers too. Until 1925 when Lewis Ryan was mayor, the old cemetery was rather uncared for. Before Decoration Day families would take sickles and sythes and clear off their plots. Lewis appointed Dewey Coffman as his special duty to clean up the burial ground. There were but two or three faucets bringing water from the Puyallup water system.

Through the courtesy of Ivan Swarthout we find that in 1902 the town section of the cemetery was added. Bill Woolery, the son of Isaac Woolery, acted as sexton for the pioneer part until the two sections were united and Sumner took over the management. Finally a six-inch water main was laid from the city limits along the Milwaukee right-of-way and into the cemetery, a distance of about a half mile.

Now having more water, even pressure was insured to all parts of the cemetery and perpetual care was given which gave Sumner and the valley one of the most beautiful burial plots in the state.

From the small beginning, two acres and voluntary labor, now the cemetery association owns 24 acres, 15 of which are not developed. Total amount in the cemetery endowment care fund to provide endowment care is $151,595.65. The interest from this provides care and maintenance to all graves sold since 1928.

This has been copied from the 1964 report of the association, and included in the history of the Pioneer Cemetery for comparison.

CHAPTER 16
MAIN STREET

The time has come to take our stroll down Main Street. It may be any time between 1890 and 1900. We will pay no attention to dates nor try to keep this walk in chronological order.

Stores began, lasted a few weeks, were sold to others, burned out or failed. The buildings were remarkable, for after the fire temporary ones were erected or hophouses moved in to be used until others could be built. They were not uniform; a livery stable might be found beside a grocery store or the bank for there was no planning for unanimity.

These were the days when the streets were muddy, few sidewalks and if there was one in front of one building the one in front of the next might be a foot higher and many a loose board tripped up a pedestrian.

But the people who lived in Sumner were like a happy family, and there was fellowship and goodwill among neighbors. Not to know the family living next door was unthinkable. Friends dropped in for a good old-fashioned visit as folks had time for friendship.

We will start across the wooden bridge at the end of west Main. In the early days canoes and horses and wagons ferried across the rivers and old settlers thought it was "wonderful" to have a bridge.

We visit with the Searles family. Voylet and her older brother and Herman with his curls and white collar. As we cross the little Stuck and look down, we think we could almost wade across it, for before the White was turned into it not much water rolled between its banks. The approach is still to be seen across the street from the Welding place. The bridge was washed out in the flood of 1906.

The first stop we will make is to watch the little smithy at his forge in the blacksmith shop. How the sparks did fly as he pounded the anvil and the way he shod the horses fascinated the children. He was so kind to them that his shop was a favorite place to spend an hour or two.

They did not know much about W. W. Smith. They would have been surprised to know that he had come from Scotland originally; that before he came to Sumner he had been a master mechanic in Fort Huron, Michigan; that Thomas Edison, then a young man, used to come into his shop and watch him work and ask questions.

Young Edison wished he had a place to experiment so Smith gave him room in which to try out his experiments. Here Edison began his discoveries which led to his announcement of the phonograph in 1877 and the introduction of electric lighting in 1878.

Henry Ford came into Smith's shop too, and the three became fast friends. When the Edison Illuminating Co. was organized Henry Ford became its chief engineer.

Henry Ford bought the Smith building when Smith came west and a plaque in it can be seen today which reads "Here Thomas Edison began his early experiment and this room was given to him by W. W. Smith."

So this was our smithy. There is an unfounded story that he became homesick for the Scotch broom in Scotland and sent for seeds, which accounts for the starting of this shrub in our valley. At any rate it still can be seen on both sides of Stuck River. His sons were Jesse and Jack, and Jesse carried on the blacksmith shop after his father's death. Jack had a barber shop and Mrs. Virgil Montagne is Jack's granddaughter. Her father was Frank Smith and her uncle Clyde, and both died recently.

Across the street from the blacksmith shop stood the Purvis home. In fact this house is still occupied. We will stop in some Sunday afternoon and join Seymour, Nellie, Spencer, Fred, Bert and Little Albert around the organ where their mother is playing and they are singing. They have visitors, for the E. Johns family lives next door and every Sunday afternoon Belle, Caddie, Helen and their cousin Amy and Rollo Everett (he is interested in Belle) would be singing with the Purvis young people.

What a mother was Mrs. Purvis! She kept her young people busy with wholesome good times. When we tired of singing, we went for walks along the river or played a game of authors, until time for Christian Endeavor at the little Presbyterian church. When the Purvis family moved to Cherry street we followed them and continued our Sunday afternoon singing. We loved the tunes where the bass and alto repeated the words.

Across the street lived the Engh family—Gertrude, Alma, Alvin, and Danny. A house had been built for Loring Sun on the John Kincaid property. This house still stands across from the Sunset garage.

After Mr. Swezey and Luella Kincaid were married and lived in the Everett house a little while they moved into this house south of the Kincaids. Their home was a gathering place for the young people. I remember a magic lantern show when Harry Ryan made the slides with Ernest Darr's help. They illustrated Clementine and we sang it as it was flashed on a sheet hung in a doorway. How we laughed when we saw her "plunge into the water!"

When Prof. Swezey, for he was now teaching languages at Whitworth College, wanted proficiency in practical use of the language, he had the class come to his home where the table was set with the dishes labled "Karofelm," "brodt," etc. We pretended to have a meal and were allowed to speak nothing but German. What a man! When Dr. Stewart, the president of Whitworth said he did not approve of Christian Endeavor, because it was a "match-making society"; back came our beloved leader with, "Where would you make better matches?" When Mr. and Mrs. Swezey took their honeymoon it was to Orilla on the train with us to a Christian Endeavor local union convention. Imagine going to Orilla on the train, today a 20-minute drive in an auto!

The schoohouse sat just south of where the Sunset garage is. If we happen in when Bert Brown had just dropped hot shot down Harry Ryan's back, we would see him jumping up and down trying to hold out his clothing to keep the shot from burning. Turning around from the blackboard Prof. Stafford is exclaiming, "Harry, what is the matter with you?" "Bert put hot shot down my neck" is the answer as he continues to dance. "Did you do that, Bert?" "Yes, sir." "Stand up. I'll attend to you." He did with an 18-inch ruler he punished Bert on the palm of his hand.

Bert Brown wrote this to Dr. Corliss who knowing my thirst for history of Sumner loaned it to me so I could copy it. Bert Brown became a Congregational minister and he said he always had trouble with that hand, finally losing the use of one finger. Doctors in Pittsfield, Vermont, said it might have come from that ruling. Punishment for discipline by the use of a ruler on the hand was common in the 1890s.

If our walk down Main Street had been after 1892 the school would have been moved to the new schoolhouse. The Dobler young people might have joined us on our stroll for they lived in a 10-room house just south of the schoolhouse.

If we arrived at the Presbyterian church on a Sunday morning, we would find Mrs. L. F. Thompson's white horse tied to the hitching rack. Perhaps she had just laid the reins over the rack and expected the old horse to stand, or she might have had a heavy weight attached to the strap which was supposed to hold him. Then he might have tired of waiting and pulled it slowly along to where some green grass looked good to him. She will find him about a block away when she comes out to go home.

As we enter we see the Stewart wagon coming loaded with George, Charley, Addison and May with their cousin Ella and Fred Craig. The hired men are there too so the Stewart group fills two pews. They were always on time, too. Margaret and Ed Stewart had married and had left home.

Miss Edmiston, the dean of women, comes with the boarding girls at Whitworth College, for attendance at church service is obligatory. Nan Duff, Amelia Loomis, Sarah Stewart, Anna Davis, Neil Patterson, Elma Longhorn, Carrie and Lena Johnson, Blanche Sargeant, Rella and Maude Wilson, Gertie Williams, Anna Hewitt, Emily Buford are usually with Miss Edmiston.

If this is communion Sunday, the elders, E. C. Meade, Willamson Stewart, W. V. McFarland, and Joseph Harris, might be passing the two large silver goblets from which every one took a sip of grape juice and broke off a piece of bread from the loaf which commemorated the Lord's Supper. These elders wore beards as did most of the men who attended church and if one looked the congregation over there were not many men present. E. C. Meade resigned as elder once because he was the only man who would serve. He always sat in the front seat by the window nearest the pulpit on the east side.

In the evening the lamps between the windows and the beautiful chandelier which hung from rosettes of plaster of paris on the ceiling were lighted. The young people had had their Christian Endeavor meeting for it was started in 1888. Mr. and Mrs. Swezey were the leaders in the 1890s. It used to bother them because a 17-year-old girl used to get the "giggles." Her cousin would say things to make her laugh and follow her from seat to seat to continue her teasing. One night Mr. Swezey gave a serious talk on reverence and it almost broke this girl's heart. She rose and said how sorry she was and never forgot the lesson learned that night. Edna Kincaid once told her she sat too "primly" in church!

When Mrs. Bailey and her son Robert and daughters Edna and Laura left for Nevada (she had been keeping house for Mr. Shipley after his wife's death), Edna wrote that they had no church service. This same "giggler" took notes on Mr. Davenport's sermons and sent them to her each week. The young people used to say that Mr. D. never looked at the congregation but out the window and preached to the hall.

It used to be the custom to have a Christmas tree in the church when a Santa came. A girl brought her four-year-old sister one night and they sat next to the aisle down which Santa pranced. As the older girl looked down she saw by Santa's brown pointed shoes that he was her boy friend. The little girl was so excited she stood up on the seat and cried out "I love Santa" over and over again ending with "Don't you love him too . . . ?", much to the embarrassment of her sister.

In the evening after church, as the boys lined up in the vestibule, the town girls came timidly out wondering if a boy would step up and ask for her company. Could it be possible that this partly accounted for so many young people enjoying church attendance? I am sure this would have been denied earnestly. Sometimes a lad sat with his favorite girl during the service and so did not have to brave the publicity of asking to see her home. Not many went steady in the gay nineties.

As we pass along the street on a weekday afternoon we might follow ladies entering the John Kincaid home across from the church. The first missionary meetings and Ladies Aid as well as parties and socials were held there.

We might have heard Al Purvis and Willie Kincaid talking as they were playmates. Al asks, "Willie do you remember how you boasted that your father was building the biggest barn in the territory?" "Yes," answers Willie, "I said that it could swallow a whole livery stable. He did it too, didn't he?"

It could have been that we passed by just after Harvey Johnson fell to his death in that barn. Harvey married Lena Baker one of the first white children born in Pierce County. Many others claimed to be first. This tragic death shocked the entire community.

In the 1890s the Harris family lived in the McCarty home across the river. They had a rowboat and many an hour Rachel and Fred and their friends spent rowing up and down the river. Parties were great fun there too.

As we enter the hall next to the church the women are busy getting ready for a social. Ice cream freezers are turning, chairs being arranged and lamps being filled. If we enter during the evening, the grand march might be starting as the first thing on the program when it is a Ladies Aid social begins with the grand march. Couples form in two lines led by Henry Wellington and Edna Kincaid, each leading a line through intricate designs, in and out until they finally come out as they began. Miller boy, skip-to-ma-loo, blind man's bluff, spin the platter and drop the handkerchief until all are tired and ready to sit down and listen to a program of singing and recitations. Ice cream and cake give a finishing relish to an evening of fellowship.

If a Whitworth College Commencement program is in progress, we will see Al Purvis busily copying the motto hung over the stage. He memorized it "*DEO-ET-HOMINI-VIVENUS*" meaning "We live for God and humanity." He carved it on a cane and when Archie Cameron saw it, he exclaimed, "That's the Whitworth Motto." "I know it," said Al. "Tell me what it means?" Archie scratched his head and couldn't remember.

The walls would echo with Robert Montgomery's orations. He was an eloquent orator and an ardent Democrat and never failed to bring forth his views vehemently. Joe Phenicie always acted out a Shakespeare drama. I can hear him yet as he gave *Hamlet*. Girls recited and a paper was read called *The Gleaner* because the best of the items in the weekly papers were used for the commencement edition. Fred Whitworth, Roy Whitcomb and I were usually the editors and I did the presentation. Later Roy Cagley and Monte Hulce were the editors. These old papers written on foolscap paper are interesting reading to old Whitworth students.

As the college had no gymnasium they rented the hall so practice by the boys was held there daily.

The section boss, Mr. Conner, lived in the house by the water talk. One could see him wheeling the handcar out on the switch main track so his inspection of the tracks might be carefully done. A party of young people often borrowed this car and rode to Puyallup on it. I have often heard Margaret Stewart Espy Bow tell of the fun they had with the handcar. How I wish we had a picture of those girls their long skirts waving in the breeze as they swept along while the boys worked it by hand.

The sidewalk in front of the section house had a railing on one side but on the other it was a six-foot drop to the ground and folks walking home from church welcomed Miss Jane Cole with her lantern guiding them past the dangerous spot near the tracks. We have told about Miss Cole in our character sketch of the well-known women of the early day.

We teenagers used to take two pins and cross them and spit on them and lay them on the track just before the train passed, then found we had a little pair of scissors when they were mashed together. This was one of the simple amusements which might be classed with the game of bum-bum-pull-away and crack-the-whip.

In our walk we will go down the track to the depot to see the train come in. We pass the newly-painted water-tank, painted because President Harrison is coming through. We hope to see him and in our hearts we secretly hope we will get a chance to shake his hand. He is a hero to us young Republicans. We had danced around bonfires shinging "Rah for Harrison. He's the man, Cleveland died in an oyster can." and "By Grover, By—Oh what makes you cry so, By Grover By—Oh, you great big duffer, Good-by." "We saw the ship go round the bend, 'Twas loaded down with Harrison men." etc.

Then the Democrat gang of youngsters would change the words and sing the same tune using "Cleveland." We just carried on what we heard at home reflecting the party to which our parents belonged. My chum was a Democrat and we remained the best of friends. We Republicans wore little jugs on a ribbon around our necks; what they stood for we hadn't the slightest idea but they had something to do with the issues of the day as did the oyster can.

Wonder of wonders, President Harrison did shake hands with us as he stood on the rear platform of the train. He didn't have a special train, just a special car. That engine had a huge cow-catcher on the front of it and we could see it as they stopped at the water tank to fill the engine boiler. I wonder if the president saw the freshly painted tank!

Beyond the depot (it was on the west side of the track) was a harness shop conducted by Mr. LeFeavor, a Frenchman. He was a very versatile man, a genius, for he painted pictures as well as carrying on a business. His walls were hung with his paintings and he had one of the president done in oils. The elk on the Shipley building was painted him.

When we come back to Main street our next stop will be at W. R. Lindsay's store. He had general merchandise and anything from calico and bombazine to china and farm implements. Two boys went to Tacoma to buy a present for their mother. They spent the whole day and found nothing, but when they came back to Lindsay's they bought a pair of beautiful Bristol glass vases, embossed with raised flowers. I own one of those vases. It paid in those days even as today to shop at home. It was in Lindsay's window that we saw the hypnotized woman, lying asleep all day. She had been brought down from the hall where the hypnotist had given an exhibition. We gazed and shivered as we remembered how he had drawn a needle and thread through her cheek. We still laughed at the way Westie Barkman went into the hypnotist's machine and came out wearing short pants, having become a boy again.

That same patent medicine man might have his wagon parked in the triangle trying to draw a crowd with his calliope. A little monkey could be seen carrying a pan for money which anyone might drop in if he didn't want to buy the medicine.

He was right in front of Wilson's Drug Store where all kinds of patent medicine might be purchased. Folks said that men who missed a saloon used to buy sarsaparilla and petuna in quantities. The tinkle of the little bell which called Mr. Wilson from the back of the store and the bottle of Carter's Little Liver Pills we bought, as well as the castor oil, will never be forgotten by the children who were sent for the "cure-all" of that day.

If it is time for the mail to be brought from the depot, people gather in the post office to wait for its distribution. While the conversation was accompanied by the sound of the hand stamp skillfully being handled by the postmaster, every eye was fastened on his box to see if any mail would be placed in it. Finally the window was thrown open and the smiling face of the postmaster appeared. It might be Tom Darr, Jake Pyles, Sam Cagley or Ernest Darr, for the same routine was followed by each.

After the mail was handed out, then confectionary, cigars or tobacco might be purchased for all post offices carried such to eke out the slender salary paid by the government.

How we wished that one of those old stampers might have been preserved and be on exhibition in the library. Pictures of Mr. Pyles, Emma and baby Phyllis in her buggy and one of Ernest Darr with his picture in the library show what the post office looked like with the hanging lamp from the ceiling.

I shall never forget the time I went to the office on Narrow Street, on my way to Sunday school when I was 14 years old. I found a big envelope addressed to me and in it was a Will from a cousin in Illinois leaving me $500.

My father was nearly distracted at that time as he had a note for $500 due at the bank and didn't know where the money was coming from. I ran all the way home, two miles, and handed him the Will. It was supposed to be for my education, supposed to be for my education but I felt that it was sent direct from God when we sorely needed it, and I walked back to Sunday school praising Him for it.

To resume our walk, we pass by the livery stable near the railroad track and hurry by as men were sitting out in front talking and we had been admonished by our mothers not to loiter near the stable. We catch one remark as we hurry by, for a man was telling how the horses screamed the night of the big fire and how hard it was to get them out of the stable.

Our next visit is to a grocery store. It might be Tom Darr's, Frank Kelly's, Will Darr's, Guffys or Henry Church's but what describes one will give us a picture of all of them. There were barrels of crackers, both thick, sweet ones and plain ones, pickles in barrels, bins of rice, bins of navy beans, bags of coffee. These were usually green beans and had to be roasted by the cook and ground in the small square mill held on her lap.

The fragrance of that cofee as it dropped into the little drawer below cannot be equaled by any coffee bought already ground. Arbuckle's coffee was a favorite brand. There were barrels of coal oil and each barrel had a spigot to turn filling the jug. Some women added chicory to their coffee to stretch it farther, when times were hard.

Big wheels of cheese on the counters were covered with cheese cloth and flies might be sitting on the cover. A wedge was cut for the customer. Bolts of calico, muslin, overalls, shoes and long black stockings for women could be found alongside the hoes and shovels.

A pot-bellied stove with fire showing through the isinglass with its spittoon usually was to be found in every store. Scales might be balanced ones with a scoop to hold the groceries. For heavy sacks of grain there were scales with weights which could be slid along and we will step on and see how much we weigh.

Jars of striped candy canes and candy hearts stood alongside jars of hoarhound candy. Boxes of long black licorice sticks and maple cigars for a penny drew children and we wonder if any are found in stores today. Girls of the 1890s collected candy hearts and vied with each other to see who could boast the largest collection.

A bandstand in the triangle with the band boys ready to give a concert attracted us as folks were gathering to listen. There we see John Darr, Conway, Tom Darr, Ray Morse, George Darr, Loring Son, Joe Stewart, Paul Paulson, Lynne Darr, Charley Stewart. Fred Lixburn and Johnny Darr tuning up, and soon, under John Darr's conducting, the concert was under way. The Darr family added much to the musical enjoyment of Sumner. A picture of this band is in the pictorial history of Sumner in the library.

Bob Soberts had a drug store in 1890 but did not last long. He advertised in the Herald always "fresh drugs." He went to Spokane where we visited him in his drug store there in the 1900s.

We join a crowd of people gathering in front of the hotel to have their pictures taken. How stiff they looked with their heads gripped in a vise behind—so they couldn't move! This hotel was run by I. T. Darr and this picture also can be seen in the library.

The Cascade Hotel, operated by D. W. Dobler in 1890, drew us to see if we could meet some visitors from other places. If we looked in later in the year we could find I. H. Scott managing it, and still later, Mrs. L. B. Murray. A hotel did not pay and Sumner often found itself without one as we were too near the city. Trains did not stop every time they went through and that kept Sumner isolated.

In the jewelry store of J. B. Kraus we peered in the window at the rings and spectacles on display. Signs told us that Drs. J. W. Hickman and E. A. Stafford, in the Ryan block, with Dr. Corliss later in the Shipley building, gave us assurance that the sick were well looked after, as these were well-qualified doctors. Drs. Mark and Stafford will be remembered as leaving Sumner abruptly.

'Tis hard to believe that Sumner had a Sumner bakery operated by A. Heller and a meat market where one could buy ice as well as meat from Hillman and Garrett.

Barber D. R. Messick advertised himself as a tonsorial artist and claimed that he gave "special attention to the dressing of ladies' hair." We are fascinated with the drawings in the architect G. C. Clement's office as he had the specifications for the new schoolhouse.

The Sumner Lumber Co., George H. Ryan, president, and E. Johns, manager, had a store while carrying on the mill at the foot of the east hill. Charles Lowe advertised a furniture store and was also a contractor and builder. He built a new schoolhouse. His daughter Jennie, still living, will be remembered by those who knew her in the 1890s.

The sound of an anvil's pounding called us to the shops of A. E. Wright and Tuel Bros. If Sumner can boast of nine gas stations on Main Street today, is it any wonder that in the early days it had three blacksmith's shops? Horses were the only means of transportation and they had to be shod and the wagons often needed repair. If our walk continued into the 1900s, we could add other smithies. Usually a water trough stood in front by the hitching rack and a cup, hung by the pump, quenched the thirst of man as well as beast. Horseshoe nails were used as nutpicks and every girl owned one.

In 1892 our family lived in the Everett house about where Corbin's is now and we could hear the tap, tap of the little shoemaker Thomas Wilton far into the night. What I believe was the first barber shop quartet used to serenade us every night, singing "In the Evening by the Moonlight" and "O Susannah" and many other songs. As they went up and down Main street they never knew how much pleasure they gave the listeners. Jack Smith and Fred Purvis were two of this quartet. We wish we knew who the others were. Could Loring Son have been one and one of the Myers boys?

The beautiful Lindsay home across the street was the center of society life and many a night we watched ladies and gentlemen arrive in their carriages to attend a gay party. This house was a mansion, with its colored glass windows, its spiral carved stairway and its lovely fireplaces, three of them opening into one chimney.

There is a fascination about this old mansion today as it stands sturdy through all these years after two movings. When Mr. Lindsay failed and his wife left for New York, the home was bought by Mr. Donnelly. When the bank building burned, Mr. Donnelly, a banker, built a small building in front of the house as a temporary place to house the bank.

For a short time the only telephone in Sumner was in this little building. It had previously been in Tom Darr's grocery store. Puyallup had but one phone, too, and they would not keep open after 8 p.m., so Tom and Al Purvis slept in his store to have the telephone available for anyone in need. Sometimes it was difficult to waken Al.

In 1897 the Elfers family lived in the Lindsay house. It was still painted an off white and though Mr. Lindsay had thought of moving it off Main Street to give way to business houses, it was not moved until 1900. There were three Elfers boys, Fred, Mert and Glen in the second and third grades when I taught in Sumner. The last I heard, Mrs. Elfers was still living in a nursing home in Wenatchee. I think all the boys have died.

The Shipley building was the most pretentious store building in Sumner and the huge picture of an elk painted on the side made it very unusual. Frank Kelley and Will Darr's grocery store and Bray and Baker's hardware and others occupied it until it burned. There was a lodge room upstairs and socials were given there. I remember attending an A.P.A. meeting in the lodge room.

Henry Church's store on the opposite corner had a large bull painted red and yellow on the entire east side, advertising Bull Durham tobacco. One woman hated to look out her window and have that picture staring her in the face. She said it spoiled the beauty of Sumner.

We have now walked past all the business section. Uncle Warren and Aunt Fanny Wood lived where the Salvation Army store is now located and the Reverend Davenport next to them. Bill Engdahl lived in that house until it was torn down a few years ago.

Rollo and Belle Everett lived about where Quality Cleaners stands and the Wolf family, Ira, Byron and George with their parents, just east of them. The Langdons occupied a large double house on the corner of Wood and Main until they moved to the home on Langdon street. The Siders family was on the northeast corner and I spent many a night there with Ethel when we both attended Whitworth College.

The Ryan farm extended to the Shipley building. A hophouse stood where the Conlon block was later built. For many years the lot stood vacant, roses climbed over the roothouse just back of it. A picket fence was put up in 1877 and a picture of the home and the hophouse can be seen at the library. Most interesting is a sketch drawn by the school teacher in 1876 showing the first buildings on the Ryan forty.

Sidewalks stopped at the Ryan's front gate and the land sloped down like a river bank to a big maple tree. where the children of the neighborhood had great fun playing in the white sand. We noted in the beginning of this narrative that the rivers in the valley changed courses and once what is now Wood Avenue was a river bed. This accounts for the sand.

The Maple tree was a favorite place to climb. As the branches were far apart a child had to be very daring to swing back and forth until reaching from branch to branch. A tree house was built and there, about 25 feet above the ground, the children spent many a happy hour. This tree grew in the barnyard which was fenced to keep the cows and horses in and a large gate gave access. A makeshift tent was erected beneath the tree and the girls played house, often begging their parents for permission to spend the night there but mothers said that home was the place to sleep.

The big red Ryan barn can be remembered by many as the Ryan farm was not built up until the town grew all around it. The barn stood right at the center of Wood and Main. Asparagus beds were still being cut across from the Methodist church long after it was built. The first of the farm to be platted was Ryan Avenue. Sumner followed, and Boyd, and then the building stopped until 1940.

Our walk will end at the Hostetter home which was where the jog in the street used to be at Meeker and Main. This rambling story of memories has been too long drawn out but that is the way the mind goes when one lives in the past. We hope it has given present folk an idea of life in the 1890s.

CHAPTER 17
HOME LIFE IN THE 1890s

One has said, "We must always have old memories and young hopes," and it is true.

Now we have taken our stroll along Main Street in the 1890s. We will go into one of the homes and see the family life in that era. It might have been any one of the homes in the Sumner community for all had so much in common.

As the kitchen was the center of life in the home we will enter the back door and find mother there. That is why the center of the home was the kitchen. Meals were prepared and served there every day as the dining room was only used when company came.

All the kitchens were large so a couch was a convenient thing for mother's rest, and a rocking chair so we could rock and nurse the baby. A walnut table, which had come with the family on the long journey west, could be extended if needed. The table was used for a study table too, as the children prepared their lessons by the light of the lamp in the center. This lamp smelled of coal oil and had to be cleaned and filled every day. Polishing the chimney was the hated chore of the girl who had to do it. Lamp light was poor enough at best so the chimney had to be perfectly clear and shining.

Scrubbing the floor which had no covering was another hard task. Women used hot Gold Dust suds and that required much rinsing. Some did this on hands and knees and had almost white floors, but it was a continual struggle.

The cook stove stood in the middle of the room and the oven was usually filled with green wood to dry; wet mittens and socks placed on it soon dried. Cold feet were warmed there, too.

At baking time the oven had to be emptied and cleaned. A black iron tea-kettle sang merrily beside the black irons left on top of the stove to keep them from rusting. The reservoir tank had to be filled often as that was the best place to get warm water, and was the nearest to automatic hot water in those days.

The big black iron kettle was the most used utensil in the kitchen. Potatoes boiled and mashed with a wooden masher were the main dish at every dinner. In the evenings often the kettle was filled with popcorn for a treat. Taffy pulls were a common event in that kitchen, too.

Families had fun together for there were no outside amusements, no radio or TV. Spelling bees with all the family taking part helped make good spellers of the children who spelled for fun.

How the children enjoyed the shadow pictures cast on the wall when father made his hands form rabbits jumping, with his fingers forming the wiggling ears.

The oil lamp had its uses in many ways besides giving light. Straight hair was curled with the curling iron hanging in the chimney for heat. Beauty parlors were never imagined in the 1890s.

The Saturday night bath was something to remember. The round wooden tub was carried in and placed near the warm stove. Qater heated in the boiler was poured in and each one took turns using the kitchen for the bathroom. Can any reader remember how one's chin rested on one's knees as he tried to sit as low as he could?

The yellow homemade soap was strong enough to get the grime off the knees and elbows. Mother's voice would come floating in from the adjoining room, "Did you remember to wash your neck and ears?" Often she would come in to be sure the small boy did get clean.

He who never took a bath in a washtub teally missed something.

When the big brown loaves of bread came out of the oven, the fragrance filled the room. A slice cut from the end of the loaf while warm and spread with fresh butter could never be equaled by any delicacy our modern cook can produce.

Mother made her yeast with hops and potatoes and often kept a "starter" from baking to baking. As the only heat in the house was a fireplace, the bread sponge was set on the warm bricks at night to ferment until morning. I have seen buckwheat batter put there to keep warm until breakfast, too.

Warming up before going to bed in the cold bedroom was a nightly habit, even undressing and carrying a hot iron to bed to take off the dampness. It makes one shiver to remember the cold beds when there was no heating system.

Back in our kitchen we see mother grinding the coffee for breakfast in the grinder held on her lap, the ground coffee dropping into the little drawer below. Fresh ground coffee was always a good cook's requirement. Arbuckle's coffee was a favorite. It came in one-pound bags and could be had green or roasted.

Can you remember the large milk pans and the thick rich cream which was skimmed off with the skimmer? It would whip with a few turns of the fork (before beaters were invented). The sour cream was churned and if you ever stood for hours pumping the dasher up and down, raising it occassionally to see if there were any flecks of butter on it, you will never forget the old churn. When the flecks appeared then a little cold water poured in hastened the gathering of the butter and you knew the drudgery was nearly over.

How good that fresh buttermilk tasted—too good to feed the pigs, but usually there was too much for family use. Many a poem was memorized by the young girl who spent hours churning and this paid off in future years.

When the skimmed milk "clabbered" soured, mother made smearcase (cottage cheese today) and, with sugar, cream and nutmeg sprinkled on top, it was considered a dish fit for a king.

Did your mother keep a turkey wing to sweep off the ashes? Could you see the glow of the fire through the grate in the little cook stove? When icing-glass was put in the front it hid the beauty of the coals through the grate.

We used to toast our bread in front of the grate, holding it on a fork. The pail of corncobs to hasten the heat of the fire stood near the stove. What delicious pies came out of that oven! Did ever pie taste as good as the ones mother used to make? Do we glamorize the past or was it our youthful appetites that added relish to the food we remember?

Pickle-making time with the smell of the vinegar and spices mingling with the odor of the onions being chopped in the large wooden bowl whet the appetite of young as well as adults.

A kitten was usually curled up under the stove, for children had to have a pet to love. It was great fun to tie pieces of paper to its paws and watch it lift each one so clumsily as it tried to walk. Mother did not let the dog in the house. A bath for a dog was unheard of and the smell of its wet hair was unpleasant, so dogs stayed outdoors.

Washday was a real day. Water had to be pumped and brought in to fill the boiler for hot water. In the winter the tub was placed on two chairs if there was no bench for it. When the hot water was ready, the corrugated washboard with the yellow soap in place, the sorted clothes were rubbed clean in their order.

The back breaking rub-a-dub-dub went on through first the finest, and on to the colored ones. Several tubs full were done before the water was changed. Then the white clothes were boiled, and they were turned several times with the clothes stick and some women used what was called a "stamper" which sucked out the dirt.

When boiled long enough, they were lifted out on the lid of the boiler with the clothes stick, which was a broom handle, and put through two rinse waters, the last one being blue. Then they were hung on the line outdoors and in this part of the country when it rained the drying on racks in front of the fireplace was some job.

Wringing the sheets so many times was hard work as before wringers were invented they had to be wrung by hand. The hand wringers were a boon to the housewife but she had to fold the garments with the buttons on the inside so they would not be torn off in the wringer.

Women did much starching of garments and these had to be sprinkled after they dried and folded until the next day ready for the arduous task of ironing with the blackirons heated on the stove. Keeping the firebox full so the fire would not go out all added to the work of getting the clothes ironed. One of the hardest tasks for the early day mother was keeping her family in clean clothes.

Most kitchens had a mirror with a comb case below it for the men to smooth their hair before coming to the table. Sometimes the same comb did duty for all, but there were exceptions to this habit.

Outside let us listen to the sounds of cows mooing, the tinkle of a cowbell, a boy calling "co-boss," to get the cows to come in to be milked. Soon we hear the milk hitting the pail as the boy sitting on the three-legged stool with his head pressed against the cow's warm side, skillfully manipulates it into the pail. If the kitten comes purring, he shoots a stream of the warm milk to it.

The sound of the pump draws us to see the priming done. Many today do not know that when the water did not come up, a little had to be poured in to prime it. Some folks had cisterns, saving the rainwater. Usually a rain barrel stood at the corner of the house. The soft rainwater was preferred for some use rather than the well water. We youngsters thought that a horse hair dropped surreptitiously into the barrel would change into a snake. It never worked any better than the superstition that a piece of the dishrag stolen and carried around the house would drive away a wart.

Now we hear the sound of a dog barking, the choo-choo of the engine and the letting off steam and the bell as the train pulled into the depot. The church bell in the evening and the school bell in the morning were familiar echoes. If we are near the hill we may hear a cougar crying and it sounds like a baby.

During the hop growing season the air is heavy with the smell of whale oil soap and quasoia chips as the hops are sprayed. If the hops are ripe, we can fill a pillow with their fragrant catkins and that will insure a good night's sleep.

The children are walking on stilts and having great fun. If we try that we may get a hard fall, it is like riding to the moon the stilts are so tall. Stilt walking is part of growing up.

Here comes a wagon filled with neighbors, which means we may be eating in the dining room tonight, getting a glimpse into the parlor where pictures of dignified men and women are hanging in gold frames, looking down on the love seat and velvet-covered chairs. They are not for us to sit on and we are glad for they are not comfortable anyway. But we may gather around the organ and sing if some one will pump it and play for us. The old organ has a good tone and we love to sing with it.

A fitting close for a description of home life is to mention the long, wool hand-knit stockings all wore and the scratching they caused. The long skirts of the women with brush braid on the bottom to keep them from wearing out as they swept the ground; the petticoats with taffeta ruffles on the bottom adding to the weight. Young women were taught how to hold up these heavy skirts gracefully even into the 1900s. The bustles holding the skirts out were usually of wire. Good old days? Maybe, but remembrance makes us appreciate the conveniences of today even in dress.

If we moralize, we can say there can still be happy family life if we take time to live and do not let ourselves be so busy that we lose the chance to have it until it is too late and our children are grown and gone. The birds always fly out of the nest all too quickly as time flies so fast these days.

We have now come to the end of this reminiscence. I shall leave the 20th century story for someone else to record. Our state has come to its 75th anniversary. Much interesting history can be written of the years since 1900. I hope the next writer of Sumner history will enjoy it as much as have I.

The following chapters were originally published in *The Seattle Times* and the *Sunday Ledger* in 1961, 1962, and 1963 and are printed here by permission.

CHAPTER 18
WHITWORTH GAVE MORE THAN HIS NAME TO COLLEGE

Whitworth College in Spokane owes, in a broad sense, a huge debt to Seattle.

A Seattle man not only inspired its inception but provided its name. And a former Seattle man, Dr. Frank F. Warren, has been its president for 25 years.

The Presbyterian college was named after George F. Whitworth, missionary, pastor, circuit rider, Indian affairs clerk and surveyor of King County and Seattle. He also had served two terms as president of the University of Washington in Seattle—from 1866-67 and 1874-76.

It was Whitworth upon whom the Rev. George A. McKinley, pastor of the Sumner Presbyterian church, called for aid in establishing a school in 1883. Out of Whitworth's efforts came the Sumner Academy, which began classes with 13 students at improvised desks in the little Sumner church which had been dedicated in 1878.

Seven years later, also through Whitworth's efforts, the academy became a college and the college building was erected in another section of the town, where it remained until it was moved to Tacoma in 1899. It was not located in Spokane until 1913.

To trace the college's struggle, first to stay alive and finally to thrive, over a period of almost a century, is to discover the determination, humor and diligence which gives a school the character to succeed.

The only Sumner school before 1883 was a two-room building, where "readin' 'ritin' and 'rithmetic" were taught. Mr. McKinley had two young sons, and a half dozen families of the area had teen-age youngsters.

Before the Second World War, the college had but two buildings housing 200 students. That was when Dr. Warren accepted the call to Whitworth, which, for him, meant leaving the security of Seattle Pacific College.

Today the college, located on the J. P. Graves estate, has 19 buildings and the prospect of two additions in the near future. Almost 1,200 of its students received liberal arts degrees the past spring. It is sixth in size of the 45 Presbyterian colleges in the United States.

If the man for whom it is named infused the college with his spirit, it will never retreat.

Born in England in 1816, George F. Whitworth moved to the United States in 1828 and was appointed a missionary to the Puget Sound area in 1853 by the Presbyterian Board of Domestic Missions.

During the winter layover in Portland, he organized that city's First Presbyterian Church. In February he established a church at Olympia and later organized the first Chehalis church in a home. Along with subsequent missionary activities, he farmed, taught, surveyed, clerked and represented Thurston County in the Legislature.

In 1860, he came to Seattle and continued preaching, teaching and surveying, while also making trips to Puyallup Valley to preach. Small wonder, then, that Mr. McKinley turned to him for help in founding the school and securing Presbyterian aid.

For an idea of the institution in those early years, listen to the report of the Sumner Herald on February 14, 1890:

> The new building is the pride of Sumner, located on a large level piece of land, fronting on the most beautiful of all the avenues of Sumner. It is a commodious structure which comprises all the modern and approved arrangements. There is also a basement story soon to be fitted up with culinary and dining compartments. The improvements will be made during the summer vacation.
>
> On the first floor is the principal's home, which includes parlor, sitting room, two bedrooms, dining room with culinary attachment. On this floor is also the chapel and general study room with seating accommodations for 125 students. The two music parlors, ln which instruction will be imparted in that art, also is on this floor.
>
> On the second floor there are two large and well-appointed recitation rooms, the matron's room, and nine students' rooms. The third floor is devoted entirely to student rooms, of which there are 16.
>
> The building throughout is finished in a manner embodying both style and comfort. It is well-plastered with hard finish and presents a truly pleasing appearance inside as well as on the exterior. The building is excellently arranged for both heat and air, there being good ventilation and good heating facilities. It is, however, proposed to arrange for a steam-heating apparatus within the present year and before the advent of another winter.
>
> Four complete courses of study are pursued at the college. They are classical, scientific, normal and musical. Thus far the latter has only been taught instrumentally; soon there will be a vocal department with a competent and efficient teacher. Mrs. A. T. Fox, a lady possessing a thorough and complete knowledge of the divine art, music, has charge

of that department. The literary department is looked after by Prof. A. T. Fox, assisted by Prof. Alex Scott. Both gentlemen are educators of experience and renown and both have degrees of M.A.

The present school year will close June 20th and reopen the second week in September.

Through the influence of the Rev. Davenport, Dr, Calvin W. Stewart from Pennsylvania was persuaded to come West and accept the presidency of Whitworth College. The catalogue of 1892 gives the instructors and their subjects as follows:

Rev. C. W. Stewart, D.D., Professor of Christian Ethics and Political Science; Rev. A. T. Fox, B.L.B.D., Professor of Moral and Intellectual Philosophy and Higher Mathematics; Rev. Wilmer McNair, A.M., Professor of Latin and German; Miss Mary Edmiston, Ph.B., Principal of the Preparatory Department; Prof. W. P. Wood, C.E., Instructor in Practical Engineering and Drawing; Miss Viola Kirkman, Teacher of typewriting, shorthand and Telegraphy; Mrs. W. L. Thompson, Teacher of Elocution. A special Ladies Course omits Greek and included music. Natural Science and Modern Language teachers will be obtained during the year.

A note of interest appears in this catalogue:

The moral tone of Sumner has a regutation above that of any city or town on the Pacific coast. It is free from saloon influences and is surrounded by a very intelligent, active and enterprising people.

The female and male students will occupy separate wings of the building and no access permitted from one to the other. Miss Edmiston, a highly cultivated and experienced teacher, will have exclusive charge of the young women, and will accompany them when necessarily called to leave the college grounds.

The young men will be under the care and supervision of the faculty while in their rooms and they will not be permitted to leave the college grounds without first obtaining permission.

The College Athletic Club is a member of the Western WashIngton Intercollegiate Athletic Association. Out of 13 prizes given for first honors in the various contests, seven were won by the Whitworth team in Seattle, May 13, 1893, They brought home the Spaulding trophy from the field meet.

In the Field Day of the W.W.A.A. held in Tacoma May 12, 1894, the championship trophy was again won by Whitworth, winning nine out of possible 14 medals.

Every Sunday morning a familiar sight was Miss Edmiston filing into church with her girls, who occupied two pews. This was compulsory. During the week she could often be seen walking the country roads with them.

In 1898 Dr. Stewart resigned and Dr. Robert Boyd, a pastor at Port Townsend, succeeded him as president.

During the depression of the 1890s, the college went through difficult times. There were less than 100 students and a large percentage of them were from the local area. These paid their $12 a semester tuition with pounds of butter, dozens of eggs, bales of hay, tons of coal and loads of wood. When this was not possible some were told to continue without paying tuition, as their attendance cost the college nothing and they were valuable students.

Every day some walked from Puyallup, rode horseback or came from Auburn on the train, which was the only means of transportation at that time. Having only calico dresses did not keep the girl day students from going on with their much desired education.

After Whitworth moved to Tacoma, he and Professor Hewitt were intimate friends. Pantry raids plagued the faculty and Professor Hewitt asked Whitworth if he couldn't give them something to put in the pies which would make the boys sick and thus they could catch the culprits. He prescribed ipecac. It worked!

A favorite saying of Professor Fox, when some one memorized a proposition in geometry, was: "That's like going down in a cellar on a dark night to find a black cat that isn't there."

Not many living can recall those days.

CHAPTER 19
U.W.'s FIRST GRADUATE HAD EXEMPLARY LIFE

Clara McCarty, for whom a residence hall on the University of Washington campus is named, was the forerunner of thousands of U. W. alumni when she stood before relatives and friends 85 years ago to receive her bachelor of science degree.

Clara had numerous distinctions in that first U. W. graduating class for she was both valedictorian and salutatorian—in fact, she was the only member of the class.

She also was the first co-ed in what was then Washington Territory and is believed to have been the first woman graduated from a Pacific Coast college.

Who was Clara McCarty? Her life bridged the pioneering past and the mature blossoming of Washington state. She was born in Fort Steilacoom in 1858, at a time when white settlers faced a threat of Indian warfare.

She died in Tacoma in 1929, 40 years after the territory had achieved statehood and long after her alma mater had become a major educational institution.

A biographical sketch of Clara McCarty actually should begin in 1852, when a wagon train of 70 wagons slowly made its way toward the new frontier of Oregon from the Midwest.

In one wagon, six motherless children rode with their grief-stricken father, William M. Kincaid. Whether the mother, Nancy Woolery Kincaid, died before the start on the journey is not known. Even where she is buried is unknown.

Ruth, 17, the oldest girl, bore the responsibility of a mother on that long journey, with the help of other women of the caravan.

Their's was the first emigrant train to go by way of Naches Pass. At one place the wagons were lowered by ropes down a grade, for the road had just been cut through the mountains.

Kincaid settled in the Puyallup Valley, where he took a donation claim and built a cabin beside the Stuck River. Deeds to property in most of what is now Sumner record that they are part of the William M. Kincaid donation claim.

A young bachelor, Jonathan C. McCarty, came West in 1854 and took a claim across the river from the Kincaids. He fell in love with Ruth. The river was no barrier to their courtship, but at first Ruth would not consider marriage as she felt responsible for her younger brothers and sisters. In 1855, however, a wedding date was set for February 12.

There was no minister in the valley, so Sherwood Bonney, the justice of peace at Steilacoom, was asked to perform the ceremony. He rode the 20 miles on horseback to the Kincaid home. On arriving, he realized that his jurisdiction extended only to the south bank of the Puyallup River, the boundary of Pierce County at that time. Since it was 30 miles to Seattle, where the couple could find another justice of the peace or a minister, the wedding was held across the river at the home of a neighbor, Robert Moore.

So that Ruth still could run across the river to attend to a little brother's needs or help her sister, Susannah, with the housework, Jonathan fixed a foot-log across the Stuck. The Stuck River then was much smaller than the Stuck of today, for some years ago the White River was channeled into it.

One day a friendly Indian came by and told the settlers that a marauding band of Indians was on its way to the valley. The next day all settlers were ordered to go to Fort Steilacoom for protection.

The women and children remained inside the fort, but the men were prepared to fight if necessary. It was while in the fort that Ruth McCarty gave birth to Clara.

When the McCarty family returned to their claim, their home had been burned, their stock had been carried away and they had to start all over again. Clara lived on the farm until she was 12. Her father carried the mail on horseback from Seattle to the valley and to Snoqualmie for eight years.

Before she entered her teens, Clara's family moved to Seattle so that the children could have a good education. McCarty became a storekeeper and Clara attended a school near what is now Second Avenue and Virginia Street. Then she had three years of preparatory work before entering the university at the age of 18.

There were 17 students who began in her class, but she was the only one to finish, and was graduated with a bachelor of science degree in June 1876.

The only senior and with but four or five juniors, Clara had the personal attention of her instructors. Formal lectures were not given and classroom periods were spent in discussion and quizzes.

Speaking of her days in the university in her later years, Clara said:

> There were less than 100 students with eight members of the faculty. About 30 students lived at home in Seattle. The 16-room dormitory housed both men and women.
>
> The tuition was $30 a year and books were shipped around the Horn from the East. Even in the '70s, about 20 students worked their way through.

Typewriters and fountain pens were unknown and even notebooks and pen and ink were scarce. Nearly all writing was done with pencil on foolscap paper.

She also told of a girls' club and a boys' club open to any one who wished to join—fraternities and sororities did not exist.

The school building, painted white and with large green shutters at every window, was at the top of a hill. A high cupola topped the roof and the four, tall Ionic columns now on the present campus adorned the front. The high-ceilinged rooms of the two stories were divided into classrooms.

The fall after her graduation, Clara McCarty taught a term in the Belltown schoolhouse which had replaced the grammar school which she had attended. The next year, as there were no railroads to the Pacific Northwest, she went to Oakland, where she did post-graduate work at the University of California. Later, she taught in the Puyallup Valley and in Tacoma.

In 1879 Clara McCarty was elected superintendent of schools in Pierce County, the first woman to hold that office. She had supervision over the schools of Tacoma, Puyallup, Sumner, Orting and many crossroad schools. One was at Wollochet Bay, one of the first schools on the peninsula. To make her tour of inspection twice a year to this school, she chartered a small steamboat.

Clara McCarty was married to John H. Wilt in 1880. Her husband died in 1907 at the age of 55. He and Clara had one daughter Clara May.

After the death of her husband, Clara McCarty Wilt continued her interest in civic enterprises, serving as a Y.M.C.A. secretary, and taking part in church and historical-society work.

Besides her University of Washington "firsts," Clara had the distinction of buying the first typewriter in Pierce County. In later years, she recalled that it was quite a curiosity and she often earned as much as $10 a day typing, an unusual amount of money for women to earn in those days.

CHAPTER 20
REDONDO—IT WILL ALWAYS BE CALLED STONE'S LANDING BY MANY OLD TIMERS

Recently while riding in a comfortable automobile, we drove down a steep hill above Redondo, catching a glimpse of the blue waters of Puget Sound. In my mind's eye, I saw loads of happy young folk riding in horse-drawn wagons, laden with tents, provisions and bedding. They were bound for a week's camping at Stone's Landing, now called Redondo. The time was the 1890s.

A visit with Mrs. Eric Jackson at Alderton had given me the early history of Stone's Landing, where her grandfather, Zacharias Stone, and his wife Jane had bought "squatter's rights" to their homestead in 1869 from Timothy Lane.

They had two sons, Samuel Phinneas and William. Their daughter, Sarah, married A. J. Oliver, whose daughter, Mrs. Jackson, has lived on the original homestead all her life.

After Zacharias and his sons had cleared their land in 1872, the sons established a logging camp above what is now Redondo and built a chute to send the logs into the Sound.

The logs then were towed to mills where they were made into lumber used to build the many homes springing up in the territory. Their family name was given to the landing when a post office was established there.

The name was changed to Redondo when Isaac Hurd and his wife took over the post office in the early 1900s. Weston J. Betts, a nephew of Isaac living at Redondo, has the original seal used to stamp "Stone, Washington Territory," on the mail.

In the 1890s Stone's Landing was the mecca for camping and picnics. I went with a group from Slaughter (now Auburn) in 1892. Also present was Ernest Van Winkle, now living at Alderton. We were led by the Rev. Jon McMillan, who had recently arrived from Ireland to be the pastor of the White River Presbyterian Church at Slaughter. He and Ernest shared a tent on that outing.

The camping was rudimentary, but very enjoyable. Some of the tents were mere pieces of canvas laid over poles. Stoves were sheet iron placed over piles of stones. Our beds were fragrant tips of fir—there were no sleeping bags then.

After moving to Sumner, I had many excursions to Stone's Landing. A week-long Christian Endeavor camp meeting once was held there, led by the

Rev. O. L. Fowler and the young minister from Slaughter. Meetings were in a huge tent at the edge of the woods, with sunrise services around a bonfire on the beach.

At night a roaring fire of driftwood was surrounded by young folks from Buckley, Puyallup, Sumner, Auburn, Kent and Orilla singing far into the night.

It was the custom to row to Maury Island to see the lighthouse. Swimming, digging clams and hunting agates made time fly. When camp broke up, we all walked up the hill to save the horses. After one such outing, six of us had to walk the 15 miles home because the driver of the team did not wait for us.

On a Fourth of July picnic in 1898, we had reached the top of the hill above Stone's Landing where a passerby told us that the Spanish-American War was over. Arthur McKinley made us stop the team to memorize every stanza of "America" before we could proceed to Stone's Landing. That was our way of celebrating.

Much of this went through my mind as we neared Redondo, now a residential district. I remember that Redondo went through the amusement-park era when there was a large skating rink, said to be the largest in the state, merry-go-rounds, slides and all kinds of amusements. After the rink burned and more homes were built on the shore, the equipment was sold to Woodland Park.

A good part of present-day Redondo is due to the efforts of Weston J. Betts, whose parents, Charles E. and Mary E., in 1904 bought 48 acres of land on which Redondo proper stands. After his father's death, Weston took over platting and improving what was left of the property. He built The Marina, a three-story structure with room for 300 boats. The boats are raised and lowered by elevators and a huge dock affords ample space for bringing boats to the marina by trailer.

Betts sold the marina some time ago and now is busy constructing a 22-unit apartment house facing the water where the skating rink once stood.

When I visited him, Betts recalled the tragedy which occurred in 1906 at the Redondo dock. A Swedish picnic had brought about 2,000 visitors to Redondo for the midsummer festival. Boats came from Bellingham, Everett, Seattle, Tacoma and other points.

The Tacoma chapter had chartered a boat which made several trips. There were about 200 passengers waiting for the last trip. They crowded the dock hoping to be first to get aboard, and about 100 went down to the boat slip below, which was held by a heavy stringer. Unfortunately teredos had bored into the wood and the slip collapsed, plunging group into the icy waters of the Sound.

Betts recalls hearing the screams for help and how planks were thrown from the dock to help those in the water. Seven person were drowned, three in one family. Many others died later from the shock and exposure.

Andrew Erikson, who lives at Mountain View above Sumner, also recalls the 1906 tragedy. He had been married in April, two months before. Erikson never fully recovered from trying to save his friends and his wife always was afraid of the water after that.

Before the automobile era ships plying the waters of Puget Sound between Seattle, Tacoma and Olympia were a common sight off Redondo. Old-timers remember the sidewheeler Geo. A. Starr, the Greyhound, the Daring, the Dauntless, the Defiance, the Dart, the Daily and the Flyer.

Redondo has changed, but the memory of the leisurely life of an earlier day still clings to its wooded hills and wave-stroked beaches.

View of Main Street Looking East, 1898.

View of Main Street Looking West, 1898.

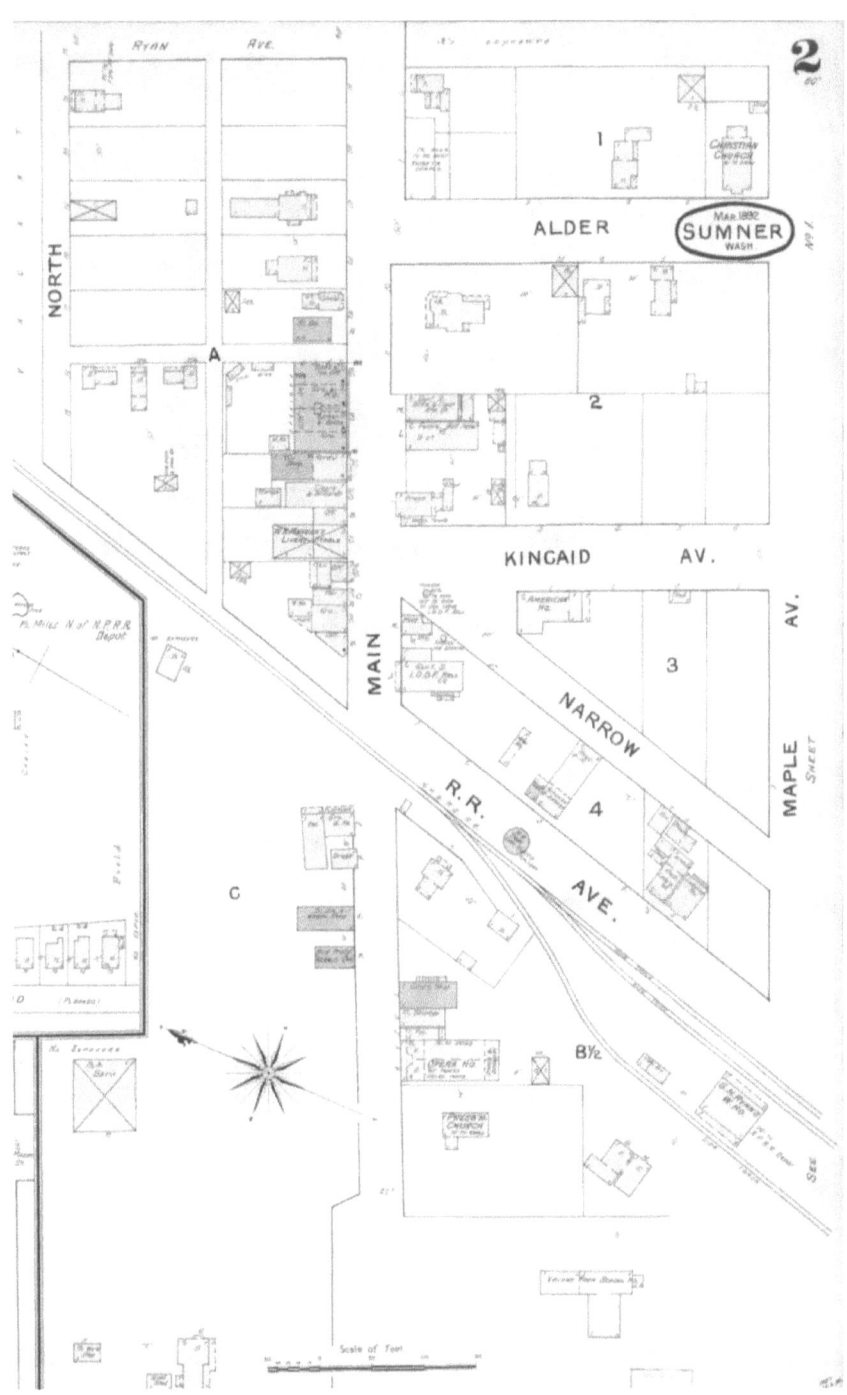

Sandborn map of Sumner, circa 1892.

Darr & Kelley Grocery.

Interior of Sumner Grocery.

R. G. Fryar's first drug store at Main and Kincaid, where The Leverenz Building now stands.

Sumner Post Office with Jacob Pyles, Postmaster, and his wife, Emma (1895).

Camping at Stone's Landing (Redondo), 1892.

Stone's Landing, 1892. Now Redondo.

Hop kiln where the hops where dried. Pickers received $1.00 for filling a bin.

Hop pickers.

Whitworth College in Sumner (1890-1899).

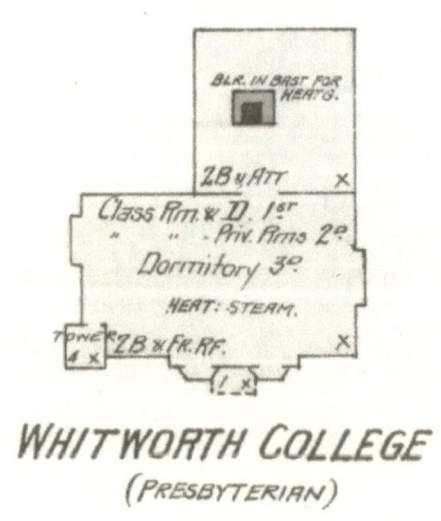

Whitworth College floor plan.

Whitworth College Football Team (1894).

Whitworth College students
on their way to an athletic meet at U of W, Seattle.

Whitworth College faculty and part of the student body (1895).

William M. Kincaid, known as the father of Sumner.
Sumner was built on his original donation land claim.

John F. Kincaid, the oldest son.

Ruth Kincaid (McCarty), the oldest daughter.

Clara McCarthy Wilt.

Laura Kincaid (Meade), Sumner's first school teacher.

George H. Ryan, Sumner's first Mayor, 1891.

Lucy Ryan and her children: Warren, Lucy, Lewis, Edith, Clarles (circa 1905).

Amy Johns (Ryan) and her second-grade class. About 1900.

Amy Johns Ryan and Edna Bailey with their bicycles (1900).

The McCarthy home north of the Stuck River.

Ryan family on the porch of the Ryan House, 1888.
This building became the Ryan House Museum in 1979.

Ryan's Mill, 1888.

Ryan's Hall. Later, it became Zech's Garage.

Sumner School, built in 1891. All grades.

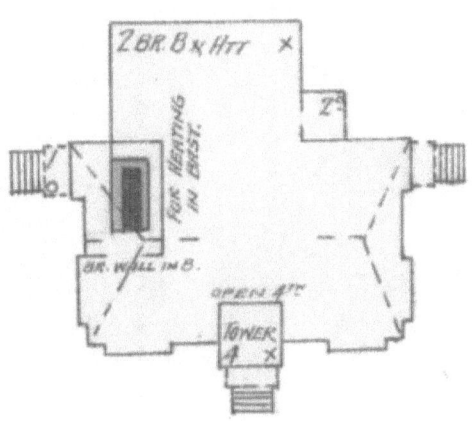

Main Street in the 1890s.

Presbyterian Church, dedicated in 1878. Sumner Academy started here.

Town Band (1895). Standing: Nall Collamore, Charley Baker, Tom Darr, Dr. Corliss, Brad Darr. Seated: Getchell, Orville Goss, Ernest Darr, Willard Goss, H. J. Trubshaw, Charley Ross.

Christian Church, on the corner of Alder and Maple.
Mr. & Mrs. George Ryan united with this church in 1879.

INDEX

Academy, Sumner, 114, 131
Allen
    A. J., 7
    Edward, 8
    Ephraim, 7
    Henry, 7
Ally, Margaret, 96
Ames
    Bessie, 77, 93
    Clara, 77
    Perly, 77
Andrews, Artemisia, 43, 61
Armour, J. C., 37
Armstrong, F. C., 80
Arney, Rev. George, 82
Arnot, Mr., 66
Atkinson, George, 59
Avery, John, 29, 25, 26, 27, 56, 57

Baker, Charley, 141
Barkman, Westie, 103
Barron, James, 7
Beckman, Mrs., 43
Beerman, Frank, 58
Bell
    James E., 96
    Debbie, 96
Benbow, L. L., 42, 81
Bergman, 65
Betts
    Charles E., 122
    Mary E., 122
    Weston J., 121, 122
Biggar, J. R., 41
Biles, James, 9

Blackburn, Frank, 35
Boatman
    John, 57
    Lettie, 21, 45, 74
    Mary Ann, 45
    Willis, 13-14, 44, 91, 94
Bock, Mrs., 43
Boice, James, 8
Bonney
    Elizabeth, 14
    Fred N., 74
    Sherwood, 14, 57, 80, 119
    Timothy, 14
    William, 57
    W. P., 11, 14, 73
Boss, Barbara, 37
Bow, Margaret Stewart Espy, 18, 101
Bowman
    Nora, 82
    W. J., 95
Boyd, Dr. Robert, 42, 81, 107, 117
Bray, Mr & Mrs., 37, 107
Brown
    Bert, 99
    W. Q., 42, 77, 78
Bryan, State Supperintendent, 80
Bryants, 37
Buford, Emily, 99
Burge, Andrew, 7, 9
Burns, Jack, 31-32
Burr
    Lynus, 95
    Mrs. Nancy, 13, 43
    Sam, 5, 57, 61
Cade, Mrs. Eugene, 11

Cagley
- Mrs. Anna, 82
- M. L., 41
- Roy, 101
- Sam, 86, 103

Cameron, Archie, 35, 101

Carson
- Frank, 74, 94
- John, 14, 95
- Vivian, 94
- Willie May, 93

Carville, W. B., 87
Church, Henry, 66, 67, 87, 89, 104, 106
Clark, Dr. Joseph, 32

Clarke
- Alice, 77
- Jennis, 78

Clements, G. C., 76
Coffman, Dewey, 6, 94, 95, 96
Cogswell, Rev. Henry, 80

Cole
- Edward, 72
- Miss Jane, 72, 102

Collamore, Nell, 141
Conner, Mr., 101

Cook
- Mrs A. E., 69
- Agnes, 79, 93
- Captain James, 7

Coombs, L. R., 38, 41, 92
Cooper, Miller, 72
Corkery, Marion, 79
Corliss, Dr., 13, 33, 81, 87, 99, 105
Cotton, C., 92

Coy
- J. J., 41
- Mr., 75

Craig
- Ella, 99
- Fred, 99

Crawford, Mary E., 79, 92

Darr
- Brad, 141
- C. M., 62, 87, 93
- Ernest, 84, 93, 98, 103, 141
- George, 104
- I. T., 37, 92, 104
- J. R., 38, 41
- John, 104
- Lynne, 104
- May, 93
- Pearl, 78
- T. B., 65, 79, 86, 89
- Tom, 103, 104, 106, 141
- Will, 89, 104, 106, 126

Davenport, Rev. D. M., 34, 38, 39 68, 75, 80, 91, 100, 106, 116

Davis
- Anna, 99
- Rev., 68

Day, B. F., 66

Dean
- Abe, 58
- George, 14

Devore, Rev. J. F., 31

Dewey,
- Governor Thomas E., 78
- Professor Henry B., 77, 78, 79, 92

Dibble, 58

Dickenson,
- Jennie, 35
- J. R., 30, 57, 95
- Mrs. J. R., 24
- Lizzie, 35

Marie Dickenson Taylor, 30
Dobler
   D. W., 93, 105
   F. S., 66
   Mrs. Priscilla, 82, 99
Doherty, Mrs. Lou, 68
Donnelly, Mr., 106
Douka, Mrs. Elva, 31
Drake, Sir Francis, 7
Driskell, 65, 76
Duff, Nan, 99

Edison, Thomas, 97, 98
Edmiston, Mary, 35, 99, 116, 117
Elfers family (Fred, Glen, Mert), 106
Elm, Mrs., 37
Engdahl
   Bill, 106
   Clara, 78
Engh family (Alma, Alvin, Danny, Gertrude), 98
Erickson, Andrew, 58
Everett
   Amy, 98
   Belle, 84, 104, 106
   Clifford, 42
   E. T., 58, 66, 92
   George, 18
   Rollo, 84, 92, 98, 104, 106
Evison, Florence, 94

Farmer, Sam, 58
Farrell, Thomas, 66
Fellender, Charles, 43
Ferguson, Lennie, 85
Fife
   Colonel Will, 69, 72, 87, 88
   Laura, 72
Filmore, President Millard, 11

Fish (Elder), 81
Fix, Bill, 58
Fogg, C. L., 92
Ford, Henry, 98
Fowler, Rev. O. L., 84, 122
Fox, Professor A. T., 35, 36, 43, 115-117
Frasure, Edward Gross, 8
Fryar
   B. S., 89
   R. G., 127
Funk, Miss Anna, 76, 79, 92

Garrett, Dwire, 42
Getchell, Mr., 141
Ghiradella, Mrs., 44
Giffy, G. A., clerk, 75
Goss
   Orville, 141
   Willard, 141
   Virgil, 67, 78
Gould, Hal, 35
Gow, Alex, 92, 96
Grainger
   Gawn, 94
   Robert, 13, 57, 92
   Mrs. Robert, 23, 24
Grant, President Ulysses S., 13
Graves, J. P., 114
Gray
   Captain Robert, 7
   Gladys Lane (Mrs. Paul), 47, 81, 92, 93, 104
   Rev., 81
Grossman, A., 59
Guffy, Mr. R. A., 36, 66
Guptil, E. T., 42
Guthrie, Inez, 42

Hall, John, 74
Harris
    Fred, 101
    Mr. Joseph, 87, 100
    Rachel, 101
Harrison, President William Henry, 63, 102
Hayward
    George D., 14, 77
    Rev. E. R., 92, 93
Haywood, George, 13
Henners, C. C., 95
Heller, A., 105
Hempstead, Ethel, 82
Henton, George E., 41
Hewitt
    Anna, 99
    Professor, 117
Hickman, Dr. J. W., 105
Himes
    George H., 10
    Tyrus, 10
Horner
    children (Blanche, Charles, Holly, Myrtle, Ross, & Roy), 42, 77
    Mrs., 43
    W. A., 92, 93
Hubbard, Olive, 78
Hueston, Hon. T., 92
Hunt, Adah, 78
Huntington, Adelle & Mirriel, 31
Hurd, Isaac, 121

Jackson, Mrs. Eric, 121
Joe, the Chinaman, 71-72
Johns
    Amy, 77-78, 84, 136
    Belle, 93

    Mrs. C. C., 69
    E., 98, 105
    Helen, 78
    Margaret, 77
Johnson
    Bessie, 77
    Carrie, 99
    Harvey, 101
    Jessie, 77
    Lena, 99

Kandle, George B., 95
Karshner, Dr. Warner, 73
Kelley
    Frank, 106, 126
    Mary, 95
    W. B., 95
Kilmer, Joyce, 64
Kincaid
    Edna, 68, 100, 101
    Chris, 10
    James, 10
    John F., 10, 15, 19, 28, 133
    Joseph, 10
    Laura, 10, 74, 131, 134
        (see also Seaman, Laura Kincaid and Meade, Laura Kincaid Seaman)
    Luella, 35, 74, 92, 98
    Nancy Woolery, 11, 118
    Ruth, 10, 135
    Susannah (Thompson), 10, 19, 21, 24, 31, 34, 45-47, 72, 99
    W. C., 93
    William M., 10, 12, 15, 16, 18, 19, 22, 74, 118, 132
    Willie, 100
Kingery, W. H., 93

Kirkman, Miss Viola, 92, 116
Kirkwood, children (Agnes, Aleck, Allen, Frances, Marian, Matthew, Ralph, Robert), 77
Kraus, J. B., 93, 105

Landin, G. L., 42
Landon, Rev. George W., 81
Lane
    John, 8, 10
    Honorable Joseph, 31
    Timothy, 121
    William, 47
Langdon
    Mrs., 43, 106
    Willis, 106
Lantz, C. R., 32, 77
LeFeavor, Mr., 102
LeMarr, Thomas, 96
Lemon, Isaac, 12, 14
Lenover
    Faye, 72
    Mable, 72
    Ralph, 72
    Tom, 62, 66
Leschi, Chief, 16
Light
    E. A., 8, 10
    Mrs. E. A., 9
Lindsay, William R., 41, 62, 102, 103, 105, 106
Lixburn, Fred, 104
Longhorn, Elma, 99
Longmire
    James, 8, 10
    Mrs. James, 9
Loomis, Amelia, 99
Lott
    Henry G., 93
    Sam, 58
Low, Robert, 96
Lowe
    Charles, 64, 67, 105
    Jennie, 105
Ludlow, Mrs., 69

Madden, W. J., 58
Maloney, Thomas, 41, 66
Manchester
    Lenora, 78
    Lydia, 89
Marble
    Blanche, 93
    Coral, 93
    H. A., 93
Mark, Dr., 105
Massey, Rev. T. J., 80
Maynard, Rev., 67
McCarty
    Clara, 74, 118-120, 134
    Jonathan C., 74, 96, 101
    Ruth, 74, 133
McCloskey, Jim, 58
McFarland
    Charles, 92
    Helen, 77
    F., 92, 93
    Kenneth, 77
    Maime, 78
    R. E., 89
    W. V., 87, 100
McGrew, James W., 42, 43
McKay, 58
McKinley
    Arthur, 35, 84
    Rev. George A., 80, 114, 115
    Ross, 35

McMillan
    D. M., 28, 42, 56
    Rev. Jon, 121
McNair, Rev. Wilmer, 92, 116
Meade
    Edith (Doll) Martin, 32
    Elijah C., 31, 32
    Laura Kincaid Seaman, 31
    Sue (Anderson), 32
Meeker
    Aaron, 13
    Ezra, 13, 16, 32, 63, 74
    Fanny, 43
    Jacob R., 13, 29, 57, 80
    John, 29, 74
    Linda, 35
    Melinda, 13
Meeks, James,
Messick
    D. R., 105
    W. R., 65
Miller, A. J., 95
Mills, John, 7
Mitchell
    Dr., 72
    William, 16
Montagne, Mrs. Virgil, 98
Montgomery, Robert, 8, 101
More
    Alice Myrtle, 95
    Charles, 95
    Edith (Herr), 19, 44, 83
    Elizabeth Smith, 44
    F. W., 58, 65
    Robert S., 7, 8, 13, 19, 95
Moore
    Mrs., 75
    Orville, 75
    Robert, 119

Morgan, Murray, 61
Morrison, Abrial, 13, 14, 80, 119
Moses, A. B., 16
Mullen, Charles, 92
Munro, Mary, 72
Murrray, Mrs. L. B., 105
Myers, George T., 42

Nichols, Miss, 75, 91
Nix, R., 13

Oliver
    A. J., 121
    Ella, 35
    Oro, 35
Owen
    Nancy, 74
    Sarah B., 74
    Thomas, 14
    William D., 74

Parker
    Angeline, 71
    Austin (Pike), 32, 77
Patterson
    Neil, 99
    Robert, 6
Patch, Rufus, 80, 96
Paulhamus
    Alice, 32
    Caroline, 32
    Clay, 33
    Dwight, 32
    W. H., 32, 65, 87
Paulson, Paul, 104
Penningtons, 37
Perham
    Adam, 14
    Addison H., 12

Phenicie, Joe, 101
Porter, John, 58, 81
Powers
    Bertha, 78
    M. C., 92
Pritchard, Rev. E. R., 80, 81, 89
Protzman, Mr., 78
Purvis
    Albert, 98, 100, 106
    Bert, 42, 57, 98
    Fred, 69, 98, 105
    Nellie, 77, 98
    Seymour, 98
    Spencer, 98
Pyles
    Emma, 103, 127
    Jake, 103, 127
    Phyllis, 127

Raymond, Mr., 59
Remington, Maria, 66
Rogers
    Connie, 85
    Oz, 74
Ross
    Charles, 141
    D. M., 95
Rousseau, A. M., 41, 80, 86
Ruel, Mr., Sr., 75
Ryan
    C. A., Sr., 5
    Charles A., 27, 135
    Edith (Van Vechten), 3, 27, 56, 135
    George H., 5, 18, 19, 22, 25, 79, 80, 92, 96, 105, 106, 107, 135, 137, 138
    Harry R., 1, 24, 27, 84, 85, 89, 99

    Lewis D., 24, 96, 135
    Lucy V., 21-23, 87, 88, 95, 135
    Warren W., 27, 106, 135

Sargeant, Blanche, 99
Sargent, Nelson, 8
Scott
    I. H., 105
    Professor Alex, 46
Seaman
    Carrie (Church), 32
    Fred C., 18, 22, 96
    Jessie (Fox), 32
    Laura Kincaid, 18, 31, 96
    Nellie (Bergmann), 32, 35
Searles
    Herman, 97
    Nathanial, 96
    Voylet, 97
Sherman
    E. M., 94
    W. W., 95
Shipley
    Grant, 63
    Levi, 63
    Mr., 75, 93, 100, 102, 105, 106
Siders, Ethel, 106
Sloan, George W., 13, 22, 80
Smith
    Clyde, 98
    Frank, 98
    Jack, 98, 105
    Jesse, 98
    Robert, 6, 18
    W. W., 86, 97, 98
Soberts, Bob, 104
Son, Loring, 98, 104, 105

Spinning
  Ben, 19, 32
  B. M., 56, 92
  Dr. Charles H., 19, 72, 73, 142
  E. Palmer (Mrs. Ben), 19, 28, 74
  Kate, 32
  Mildred, 73
  Mrs. Will, 86
Stafford
  Dr. E. A., 65, 92, 105
  Professor, 99
Stevens, Governor Isaac, 22, 44, 73
Stewart
  Addison, 84, 85, 99
  A. W., 60
  C. E., 59
  Dr. C. W., 63, 81, 95, 99, 116, 117
  Charley, 35, 99, 104
  Ed, 99
  Mrs. E. J., 43
  George, 21, 99
  Joseph, 42, 104
  J. P., 95
  Margaret, 99
  May, 84, 99
  Sarah, 99
  Williamson, 42, 100
Stone
  E. S., 94, 95
  Jane, 121
  John, 57, 95
  Samuel Phinneas, 121
  Sarah, 121
  William, 121
  Zacharias, 82, 84, 95, 121, 122, 128, 129
Sumner, Charles, 18

Swarthout, Ivan, 96
Swenson, F., 62
Swezey
  E. D., 5, 68, 69, 81, 92, 95, 98, 99, 100
  Mrs., 22, 72, 92, 95, 99, 100

Tait
  Professor Leonard, 75, 76, 91
Thayer, Mrs. R., 79
Thompson
  Edwin Meade, 19
  Estella, 19, 35
  Fred, 65
  Hazel, 42
  Laura, 72
  Levant F., 13, 18, 19, 31, 34, 45-48, 57, 62, 75, 95
  Susannah (see Kincaid, Susannah)
  William L., 41, 65, 67, 92
  Mrs. Will, 92, 116
Trubshaw, H. J., 141
Tuel
  John, Mr., 78, 92, 104
  Myrtle, 93
Tull, John, 93

Van Buren, W. D., 8
Vancouver, Captain George, 7
VanFliet, Frank, 87
VanTassel, 77, 85
Van Vechten, Dr. Ward, 27, 35
Van Winkle, Ernest, 121
Vining, Mr., 28, 50, 56

Warren, Dr. Frank F., 114
Watson, J. G., 80

Weisner, Essie Williams, 45
Wellington
    A. G., 69
    Carrie, 92
    Henry, 68, 69, 92, 101
    Mary, 75, 76, 91, 92
Whitcomb, Roy, 101
Whitesell
    Alex H., 94
    Elizabeth, 47
    George W., 94
Whitworth
    Fred, 101
    Dr. George F., 19, 21, 34, 38, 48, 60, 68, 80, 114, 115
Wigton, Jim, 71
Williams
    dentist, 65
    Effie, 94
    Dr. Fred, 14
    George, 94
    Gertie, 99
    Henry, 38, 41, 60, 94
    Herbert, 14, 32
    John, 94
    Lettie Boatman, 21, 75, 94
    Lucy, 94
    Millie, 94
    Sydney, 14, 32, 77
Wilson
    Maude, 99
    Newell, 35
    Rella, 99
    W. W., 66, 103
Wilton, Thomas, 49, 105
Wilt, John H., 120
Wood
    Charles, 28
    Fanny, 107
    J. W., 88
    W. P., 57, 85, 86, 116
Wolf
    Byron, 106
    George, 106
    Ira, 106
Wolff, W. W., 92
Woodside, Henry, 58
Woolery
    Abraham H., 10, 13, 14, 16, 60, 72, 74, 87, 95
    Agnes, 10
    Alice, 94
    "Aunt Pop", 10, 13, 95
    Bill (son of Isaac), 96
    Daniel, 10, 74
    F., 95
    Isaac, 10, 13, 44, 95, 96
    Jacob Francis, 10, 74
    James M., 10
    Johnny, 74
    Lydia, 74
    M. A., 95
    Mary (wife of Isaac), 10, 94
    Nancy (Kincaid), 11, 118
    Robert L., 10
    Sarah Jane, 10
    William H., 74
Wright
    A. E., 66, 105
    B. F., 18, 80
    Dave, 58
    Hansford, 67
    Israel, 18, 19, 80
    James H., 28, 57
    J. C. "Dock", 58
    Nancy, 18
    Phylander, 58
    Rebecca, 18

T. A., 58
Thomas, 80

Young
Emma, 71, 74, 78
E. T., 81
Frank, 71, 81

Zech, Don, 18, 19, 70, 138

www.ingramcontent.com/pod-product-compliance
Lightning Source LLC
Chambersburg PA
CBHW060527080526
44586CB00012B/646